Praise for *The Last-Minute Party Girl*

"Erika divulges all her tips, secrets, and social etiquette in *The Last-Minute Party Girl*. This ultra-hip book is all an aspiring hostess needs to throw a successful party. Infectiously upbeat and bursting with easy-to-follow recipes, one can finally whip up a party like the pros do. All parties should be this easy and fun!"

—THOMAS KELLER ✳ chef/owner, French Laundry restaurant

"Even the most experienced party planners will find *The Last-Minute Party Girl* packed with cool ideas. This book tells it like it is and breaks all the traditional rules of entertaining. I'm amazed at how many great ideas are included in one little book."

—ROBERT ELL ✳ talent executive, Style Network's "You're Invited"

"Erika Lenkert's recipes for tossing fabulous parties are equal parts sexy, sweet, spicy, and sassy. With hilarious stories and an insider's approach, *The Last-Minute Party Girl* is the ultimate handbook for hosting the perfect party."

—PETER DAVIS ✳ editor at large, *Paper* magazine

"Leave it to a party goddess like Erika Lenkert to put out a how-to book that's actually fun to read. *The Last-Minute Party Girl* is a must-have for every helpless hostess—packed with secrets on how to pull off a swank affair and look cool while you're doing it."

    —MAILE CARPENTER ✳ food editor, *Time Out New York* magazine

"*The Last-Minute Party Girl* puts the *fun* back into *fun*ctions. It's a lively resource for those who like to entertain with style but don't have the time (not to mention the pocketbook) to turn a simple soiree into their raison d'être for a month."

    —GLYNIS COSTIN ✳ party girl, mother of two, and West Coast bureau chief, *InStyle* magazine

"Erika's advice and carefree attitude toward entertaining remind us to relax and enjoy the magic that happens when we celebrate with great friends, wine, and food."

    —ROBERT AND MARGRIT MONDAVI ✳ Robert Mondavi Winery

"The 'Sex and the City' generation can dish out pantry advice as well as any seasoned home economist. *The Last-Minute Party Girl* proffers tips on entertaining, cooking, and saving money with the cheeky insouciance of Sarah Jessica Parker's TV persona."

    —*Boston Globe*

The Last-Minute
Party Girl

Fashionable, Fearless,
and Foolishly Simple Entertaining

ERIKA LENKERT

Contemporary Books

Chicago   New York   San Francisco   Lisbon   London   Madrid   Mexico City
Milan   New Delhi   San Juan   Seoul   Singapore   Sydney   Toronto

*The **McGraw·Hill** Companies*

Library of Congress Cataloging-in-Publication Data

Lenkert, Erika.
    The last-minute party girl : fashionable, fearless, and foolishly simple entertaining
/ Erika Lenkert.
        p.   cm.
    ISBN 0-07-141192-5
    1. Entertaining.   2. Cookery.   I. Title.

  TX731.L394   2003
  642.4—dc21   2002041487

2 3 4 5 6 7 8 9 0 AGM/AGM 2 1 0 9 8 7 6 5 4 3

ISBN 0-07-141192-5

Interior design by Monica Baziuk

McGraw-Hill books are available at special quantity discounts to use as premiums and
sales promotions, or for use in corporate training programs. For more information, please
write to the Director of Special Sales, Professional Publishing, McGraw-Hill, Two Penn
Plaza, New York, NY 10121-2298. Or contact your local bookstore.

This book is printed on acid-free paper.

Contents

Acknowledgments

The hugest of party-girl hugs to my mother, Faith Winthrop, a tireless sous-chef, cheerleader, and party woman—even if she never has hangovers—and the person who taught me that cooking for others is one of the best ways to spend time with people you love and to show them how special they are. Endless double-handed air kisses and full-lipped smooches to the chefs, restaurateurs, and wine makers who have fed me so well over the years and demonstrated that true hospitality has nothing to do with stuffiness or taking yourself too seriously. Top of my list are spectacular chefs and friends who contributed to the deliciousness of this book: John Ash, Aimee Lee Ball, Carrie Brown, John Clark, Dana Cowin, Sue Diodati, Lissa Doumani, Wendy Downing, Jay Frank, Kenny Fukumoto, Sarnsern Gajaseni, Suzanne Goin, Sarah Klein, Laurent Manrique, Michael Mina, Lisa Minucci, Jean-Paul Picot, Gayle Pirie, Alfred Portale, Wolfgang Puck, Tamanoon Punchun, Richard Reddington, Donna and Giovanni Scala, Marika Shimamoto Doob, Annie Somerville, Hiro Sone, Craig Stoll, and Phillip Weingarten. A special shout-out to fellow writers and adventure companions Aimee Lee Ball and Laura Chamorro for encouraging me to be fearlessly fun with this book. Likewise Sue Furdek, Steve Kirsh, Charlotte Milan, and my mom for tirelessly poring over pages and recipes with me, my agent Noah Lukeman for watering my ego when I was wilting, and my editor Denise Betts for great guidance and encouragement. Finally, an open-mouthed wink to my pals past, present, and future who continue to show up at my parties with an insatiable appetite for food and friendship.

Introduction

The party girl has a passion for shamelessly celebrating life. She knows that the secret to a fantastic party is not filet mignon, French champagne, and designer digs but a hearty dash of graciousness seasoned with style and flavor and sprinkled with good friends. She also knows that a fabulous party doesn't require days of preparation. Not that spending a few hours elbow-deep in pastry dough won't add extra pizzazz to the night's fete, but the successful go-girl plans her limited time wisely and rarely has the time to slow-roast a pork butt or hand-make spinach pasta. So, how does she manage to throw together yet another stunning affair in a few hours with nary a bead of sweat cresting on her sculpted brow? Welcome to the world of *The Last-Minute Party Girl*, the ultimate guide to fashionable, fearless, and foolishly simple entertaining. With superb recipes (including some from the nation's top chefs), tips on cutting costs and time, theme menus, cocktail cues, two-second tricks to seduce all the senses, and invaluable advice on how to be perfectly gracious, last-minute party girls around the world are always first in party planning *and* having fun at their own fiestas.

Whether you can barely boil water or can whip up a world-class meal, this book gives you every reason to put on an apron, perk up your sense of adventure, and let your inner party girl—or guy—out to play. You can stay safe with effortless recipes and ready-made items or push the party-girl envelope with straightforward but more adventurous treats. It's all good, it's all in good fun and great taste, and it's all about having a blast and making memories around your celebrations. Play your party-girl cards right and even when you get the air knocked out of your soufflé, you'll remember the most important party-girl secret of all: Everything has memorable flavor when it's made from the heart and served in comfortable surroundings among friends.

Now, party on.

Party Girl Etiquette

WHEN I WAS in my late twenties, my mother and I attended a groovy Los Angeles wedding. The bride and groom married at the Self-Realization Fellowship Lake Shrine, a meditative park with a gilded temple, spiritual scene, and the glistening Pacific Ocean beyond. Later we migrated to an equally Zen restaurant for an organic vegetarian feast alongside a babbling brook. My mother and I were seated with three unfamiliar women, one of whom I had spied meditating under a tree before the ceremony. She had an extremely earthy quality and was nice enough, but more important, she did the most incredible thing I've ever witnessed at a dinner table. After finishing her salad slathered with green goddess dressing, she quietly picked up her plate and in long, wide-tongued strokes licked it clean. Dumbfounded, I kicked my mom to make sure she bore witness. Almost ten years later I still delight in that vignette, partially because it was so wonderfully shocking and partially because I admired her. She loved the salad, wanted to enjoy every last lick of it, and did so unabashedly. There's something to be said for people who don't let silly formalities stand in the way of pleasure. Today I'm still in the camp that believes public plate licking is about as tasteful as chewing with your mouth open. But I must admit that on rare occasions my private parties have included tongue-to-plate tactics. Truth is, proper party-girl manners depend on who's looking, so know your audience before you balance the soupspoon on your nose.

*

A polished party girl knows that the true secret to entertaining is not something she can pop into her shopping basket or borrow from a neighbor, but rather a sense of enthusiasm and graciousness that goes into everything from her inspiring invitations and party manners to giving thanks. Follow the particulars of "Party Girl Etiquette" to add a thoughtful and detailed spin to all your party plans.

* Inspiring Invitations

Think of your invitation as an advertisement for a blockbuster movie. As a preview of the shindig, it tells your guests whether they have to race to RSVP for opening-night tickets or can wait until it goes to video. Desperately last-minute phone calls aside, invitations can be postman delivered or E-mail announcements. Whatever method you choose, to get the party started the second your guests know they're on the list, you must deploy details with panache. Follow the format here—or the What, When, Where, How, and Embellish—to add Mel Gibson–like suspense, a little Julia Roberts–style leg, or Mike Myers slapstick to your party announcement.

What

The "what" is the theme of your party. Determine whether it's a dinner, brunch, birthday, baby shower, intimate gathering, BYO buddies bash, costume party, cocktail stopover, casual event, or formal affair. Be as specific as you can and write down words that describe your party vision. My casual events conjure words such as *kickin' it, chillin', festive, libations, snacks, BYO barbecuables,* and *lounge*. Words such as *cordially invited, cocktails, refined, hors d'oeuvres, elegant, dine,* and *spaghetti-strap dress* say more formal. For a pool party I come up with *splash, Marco Polo, float,* and *sarong*. (Alas, I'm too coy for Sisqo's "thong-th-thong-thong-thong.") Revisit your list of words when framing the "when," "where," and "how." I don't end up including all the descriptors in my invite, but they help me to shape the image I'm trying to portray and set the tone for my guests and me. Incorporate playful banter into your invite to get the party started right.

Look over your descriptive words and create a title for your party that captures its essence. For a pool party I titled my invite "Free Swim." A Thai food buffet luncheon and Thai margarita party was "Thai One On." A landmark birthday? "Cold Kickin' It Live at 25." Over-the-top party boy, Hollywood producer, and friend Robert Ell got more than one hundred of his pals to hit Vegas bars wearing Afros for his "Afrodesiac" party. Make your title catchy and fun, and support it with words to match.

When

Now address the "when," or time frame. Time tells more than just when people should arrive. It also sets guests' expectations. Throw an event at 7:30 P.M. and everyone will anticipate dinner. Start the festivities at 3 P.M. and people will assume they should have lunch beforehand. Have a morning hoedown and you'd better be serving coffee and at least a morning snack. Also, depending on the purpose of your event, your guests may see the start time as important only in conjunction with the end, or the window of prime party time in between, so plan your schedule wisely and add an end time. It tells guests whether they need to be punctual for the cutting of the cake (like a 3 P.M. to 6 P.M. birthday party) or can straggle in two hours after the glasses start clinking (a party from "8 P.M. to whenever"). Promptness isn't essential for an all-night rager or all-day barbecue, but it is for a surprise party or sit-down dinner. If you give guests the flexibility to saunter in a few hours late, they will, so either anticipate staggered arrivals and departures or specify otherwise. Plan your times right and people won't call you wondering whether or not they should eat beforehand, and won't show up just in time to help you do the dishes.

Where

"Where" is straightforward, but critical. Give the address and phone number, and include a map if you're inviting people who aren't familiar with your location. Some online invite sites such as very cool Evite.com offer a link to MapQuest.com, which will guide your guests from their pads to yours. If you're sending announcements by snail mail, print out a MapQuest.com map or photocopy any map, write out directions, and include a page with both visual and written details. No go-girl wants to stop mid-martini to act as party traffic controller.

How

The "how" is your opportunity to get guests involved, tell them any additional information they need to know, and request specifics like RSVPs. Want each person to bring a bottle of wine or a six-pack of brewskies? Say so. Requesting no presents at your birthday party? Note it now. Need to build your martini glass or CD collection? Title your party "Martini Madness" or "Sing for Your Supper" and tell guests to come armed with a donation cocktail glass or their favorite obscure CD. I've requested guests to don finger puppets for Halloween, bring a dish for a potluck party, and arrive with towels and bathing suits so I wouldn't end up with a nudist pool party and lots of laundry. This is also the time to note if guests can bring their posses or should arrive solo. Make it clear and always request RSVPs. It's the only way to anticipate whether you can get by with your beverage-service supplies or need to recruit rocks glass reinforcements.

Embellish

Now that you have an outline of the details, embellish them by determining the most stylish way to package your invitation. Internet invites (see the following paragraph) are perfect for the last-minute party girl, but they are no substitute for the real postman-delivered thing. If you've got a few weeks and a budget for stamps, envelopes, and whatever you put inside, put your party-girl thinking cap on and conceptualize an unusual way to tell your party people how fab this fete will be. Having a beach party? Send a deflated beach ball or a flip-flop with the vitals written on it. Hosting a cocktail party? Send a swizzle stick with instructions on how to swap it for a stiff one. Getting a group of friends together? Buy a Barrel of Monkeys. (Remember the kids' toy where the red monkeys' arms link to form a chain? They're about $4 and available online.) Send one of the monkeys to guests, and tell them they're encouraged to hang around. I've announced a picnic with a baggie filled with plastic ants, a plastic fork, and a piece of a plastic gingham tablecloth penned with the particulars, and a birthday party with paper donkey tails that promised a rousing round of the childhood classic pin the tail on the donkey. Stay away from preprinted cards, which take all the fun out of the formalities. As you put the final touches on your information and transfer it to your invitation, try to use words that reinforce your event's theme.

Internet invites don't allow for four-dimensional frivolity, but they are a dream for the spontaneous, budget-minded, or just plain lazy party girl. After you've added verve to your verbiage by following the preceding guidelines, go to Evite.com (www.evite.com), follow the prompts to custom create a virtual invite, and E-mail your announcement to your party peeps. You can also send a simple group E-mail, blind-copied to protect the privacy of your party pals, of course.

Party Favors

Your efforts are enough of a gift. But if you want to give your guests something fun for the road, you don't have to spend a lot of money. Be creative. Buy 25¢ toys in plastic bubbles, the kind in vending machines that tempt tots at most supermarkets. Make Chocolate-Dipped Desires (see Chapter 9), wrap your sweet treats in plastic and then in tissue, and tie them with a bow. Stop by a toy store and stock up on mini Slinkys, or send people home sucking See's lollipops (see the Resource Guide for details). Buy sea salt in bulk, season it with aromatherapy oil and lavender, package it in individual to-go bags, and include a rubber duck or plastic bath toy. Or hand each guest a temporary tattoo. For the party girl, playfulness scores big points, even when you're waving friends out the door.

Party Girl Gifts

The party girl should always be ready for the unexpected, including when she's forgotten to buy a gift and the intended recipient is on his or her way over. This is why I stock up on stylish $20 to $50 knickknacks (such as candles, rubber ducks, cute coasters, sexy salt and pepper shakers, and beautiful baby gifts). They're usually things I want for myself but don't need, which gives me the satisfaction of purchasing them without buyer's remorse. Now when friends arrive at my house and they've got a newborn in tow, they've just blown out their birthday candles, or they need a little retail pick-me-up from go-girl blues, I pull a pretty present out of the closet. To build a gift stash of your own, check out the Resource Guide at the end of the book for some of my favorite suppliers that can ship directly to your front door or the recipient.

Clothing Optional

As the hostess, you're in the unique position to be as fashionably flamboyant as you wish. I've donned a tutu and tiara, cocktail dresses and candy necklaces, swimsuits, flip-flops and finger puppets, and skirts with superspiked heels. One of my favorite examples of the well-dressed party person is Dana Cowin, editor in chief of *Food & Wine* magazine. When I first met her, she was dressed in basic black and draped in a stunning bright orange Indian sari, which I later learned doubles as a tablecloth. Every time I've seen her since, she's always wearing one dramatic piece that's elegantly eye-catching. When you're the belle of the ball, dress how you want. Go sexy in a clingy shirt and slacks. Slip on a tiara with your T-shirt and jeans. Add some sizzle to your all-black attire with a burgundy boa, or say sophistication with a sleek cocktail dress. Or do as Dana does and add one very special item to your event attire. At your own party you set the regalia rules, so be fearless and fun with your fashion.

Party Manners

Go-girl manners are not about refraining from licking your fingers or spontaneously dancing during dinner. The only essential task for the proper party girl is to make every guest feel important and welcome from the moment they air-kiss hello to when the designated driver drags them out the door. As the party's ambassador, you can easily spread goodwill and graciousness *and* successfully misbehave if you mind the following midparty musts.

Must-Have Munchies

Make no mistake. Even if you're having a "cocktail party," you must have some kind of foods sprinkled around the soiree—if for no other reason than to keep your guests from taking a midparty nap in your bathroom or bedroom. Check out the "A-List Appetizers" in Chapter 5, and hopefully the only spinning going on at your party will be that of two turntables and a microphone.

Coat Check

The first obvious difference between fine restaurants and the corner bistro is how diners are greeted when they walk in the door. Give your guests five-star service. Take their coats and purses and place them in a designated coat area that's not in the center of the entertaining action. Let them know where it is so they can locate their lipstick whenever they choose.

Introductions

Make sure you announce new arrivals. If you're throwing a petite party, you should make the rounds, ensuring that everyone has met. For larger fetes, present your pals—using either first names only or both first and last if you remember them—to at least one cocktailing cluster before flitting off to the next group of newbies. I am terrible at remembering names, but that doesn't deter me from being a considerate hostess. I either apologize for my absentmindedness and ask again (the best way, because no one cares and it's obvious when you've forgotten anyway), find a friend who can remind me, or wing it by tossing the unknown person into the mix and encouraging people to introduce themselves.

Potpourri for the Palate

We live in a complicated culinary time in which vegetarians and vegans mingle with meat eaters and hungry souls suffer from wheat, garlic, and lactose intolerance. Make sure all your partying palates can partake: serve a well-rounded selection of vegetables, vegetarian spreads, cheeses, and carnivore favorites and the bases should be well covered.

Mess Management

Remember, you're the host, not the maid. After the event you'll need to seek out cups stashed in places that make you wonder what your guests have been up to and scrub unknown sticky substances off your kitchen floor. But during your fete you should always dis the dishes and stay focused on fun with your friends. Put a garbage can or two in plain view so people can clean up after themselves. Make a clean sweep one or two times over the course of the party, but save the serious sponging for after the stragglers have hit the streets. The gracious party girl always puts people before her pots and pans.

Don't Dis Your Dinner

Even when the salmon's charred and the salad is too salty, don't apologize for your food. It's unsavory to bring criticism to the table—even when it's self-loathing—and it's not going to make the food taste any better. Instead, focus on the flavor of the evening—the conversation, the wine, and sharing time with your friends.

✳ Party Talk

As far as I'm concerned, the racier the conversation, the better. But after years of sitting through all types of party chatter, I've created a shortlist of no-no's, all of which are negotiable depending on who's within earshot.

For example, I learned the hard way not to chat up my conservative father with tales of taking my married male boss to a strip club. (Oops.) More universally inappropriate banter includes talking smack—saying something bad about someone—which casts a black and bitter cloud over even the brightest of go-girls, and any discussions of cats, dogs, children, or politics. These topics are contagious and deadly. People are usually vehemently opinionated and will bring down the soiree spirit trying to pump up their perspectives. I've seen the dog-versus-cat debate start at one table in a restaurant, jump to nearby diners, and create a flurry of pet peeves. Besides, even if you're sitting with a table of cat lovers, no one cares to learn the details of how Fluffy pokes your face when she wants you to wake up. Finally, keep the topics inclusive. Even my practiced circle of go-girls has a hard time steering clear of chick talk, which sends our straight male friends careening toward the TV for a sports update. Keeping the word up is especially important at the dinner table, where everyone's a captive audience. As the hostess, you are responsible for making sure everyone's in the gossip mix, so survey the scene and orchestrate the chitchat as necessary.

If your party's intimate, you can stimulate deep—or juicy—conversation by posing a pertinent question to your posse and asking everyone at the event to answer. Questions that have worked their way around my dinner table include "What is the most embarrassing moment of your life?"; "If you could experience one moment in your life over again, what would it be?"; "What are the most important events of your life?"; and "What is something important that people should know about you?" Call it grown-up truth-or-dare without the kissing in the closet. Or, what the hell—play truth-or-dare like the good old days.

✳ Giving Thanks

Expressing gratitude is a lost and greatly underrated art and an absolute must for the classy go-girl. When someone gives you a gift, hosts a dinner, helps in the kitchen, or works it in your favor in the workplace, there is no better way to acknowledge the gesture than with a handwritten, personalized thank-you card. It's sad that people don't do it more often, but on the bright side, your gift of graciousness will seriously stand out. Buy a few boxes of blank cards to keep on hand so you don't get swept away with the go-girl life before giving props to your pleasure providers. Spell out the details of how much you loved the birthday bouquet, the grilled salmon spread, or the support with pizza prep, stick your sentiments in the mail, and you're as good as solid gold. At the very least, make a call or send an E-mail. If someone does something really special, take it a step further and send the person a gift. (See "Party Girl Gifts" earlier in the chapter.)

✳

I HAVE A theory that people spend about five seconds paying attention to others and then they go back to thinking about themselves. This notion is especially reassuring during life's embarrassing moments, including when I've put my foot in my mouth in a social situation and the scene replays itself in my head like a skipping CD.

My favorite example of a serious verbal fumble was when I was twenty-one years old and visiting my conservative father and his wife. It was a formal dinner affair—candles burning, minipumpkins and leaves decorating the table, and careful conversation with my stepmother and father, whom I really wanted to impress. My dad's wife was serving fish and asked if I liked seafood. I told her yes, adding that it had not always been the case, especially in regard to calamari. When she asked why, I confidently answered, "I've never liked the idea of testicles in my mouth." During a very long pause I wondered whether I'd said something wrong and then settled on the notion that *testicles* is one of those words that has two meanings. Conversation continued, but for the rest of the night I felt an unidentifiable sense of dread. At 3 A.M. the following morning I jolted out of bed, realizing *testicles* was a very different word from my intended *tentacles*. I called my mother in horror. "Mom," I exclaimed, "I told Dad I don't like testicles in my mouth!" My mom is great at many things, one of which is soothing panicked moments—even when it's 3 A.M. "That's OK," she said. "For some people it's an acquired taste." Even now, that faux pas is huge for me, but according to my stepmother, it isn't for them—she had no recollection of the event. The point is, everyone makes an ass of himself or herself from time to time. If you say or do the wrong thing at the dinner table, forgive yourself and move on. If an apology is in order, offer one immediately and your mind won't be reliving the event for the rest of the evening. In seriously offensive scenarios remind yourself that the worst blunders later make for the best dinner-table tales.

2

Vibe by Design

I'M ALWAYS ON the lookout for fun things to add to my bag of entertaining tricks. While writing this book, I took a café break and stumbled upon $1.50 "sparkling candles" next to the register. (Think sparklers with wax.) For me some of life's greatest joys are novelties like French pedicures, minuscule bouquets of wildflowers, and, on this particular morning, sparkling candles. I didn't have any birthday parties planned, nor did I intend to entertain until this manuscript was done, but as I forked over the extra cash with my nonfat latte and tucked the spaghetti-thin tapers into my purse, I imagined the scene from *Sixteen Candles* when Jake woos Samantha with a very romantic first kiss over a birthday cake. (Even two decades later, that scene brings out the hopeful lovelorn teenager in me.) Suddenly I'm thinking about a future romantic interlude and how to integrate food fireworks. At the very least, I'll tuck the candles in a drawer, forget about them, and rediscover them right when I need them. When you're out in the world, train your eyes to scout out novelties. When the lights are dimmed and the wick is lit, today's trivial item could be the key ingredient for turning a scoop of ice cream into a storybook moment.

*

The vibe is the key to a killer party. You can fill your friends with gourmet food and wow them with designer furnishings and dishware, but even my most persnickety chef friends concede that the real party requirements—aside from quality guests—are a comfortable space, atmospheric lighting, and great music. You don't need to spend a fortune to create a romantic interlude for two or a disco inferno for a hundred. But you do need to make your space party friendly.

If you haven't put heart into your home decoration, two hours before a party is not the time to start. But there are a few things you should do—in advance or ten minutes before the bash begins—to give your pad some party-ready pizzazz.

Let There Be Controlled Light

Aside from a few cocktails, a warm glow is the most surefire way to put everyone in a better light. Before the guests arrive, I always survey my light sources. For evening events, avoid using bright overhead lights other than in the kitchen where you need to see straight. Turn on lamps, light candles, and, if you haven't already, invest in dimmer switches. They create a world of options between disenchanting direct light and complete darkness and are perfect for the dining room, living room, and even the bedroom should the go-girl's most private parties parlay themselves there. If you can't be bothered with working out the wiring, no doubt you're crafty enough to call on a friend who has the tools and the gumption. You can also buy lamp dimmer switches that require no wiring, cost around ten bucks, and are available at most hardware stores. At the minimum, screw in a few low-watt bulbs rather than casting an unattractive glare on your soiree.

✳ Waxing Romantic

Tea lights, tapers, and big sculptured candles bring a sense of drama to your dinner. They can also stage a saga for your pocketbook, so buy them in bulk from discount stores whenever you can.

Tea lights are the Mini-Me's of candles. The tiny aluminum-encased waxed wicks usually sold in bulk are cheap and romantic and can set the mood with a flick of the lighter. Arrange them en masse in strategic locations or line them up across your dinner table to cast your guests in a warm, sultry glow.

Tapers wax formal, standing tall and thin in candlesticks, candelabras, or sconces. They also have a tendency to drip on your favorite tablecloth, can create mayhem on the carpet, and have a curious way of inspiring guests to annoyingly pick at the dried puddles. Avoid the hassle. Buy dripless candles so that your flame of focus is that hottie sitting across from you. Or make your candles dripless: soak them in a strong saltwater solution for a few hours, let them dry, and then burn, baby, burn.

Block, pillar, and other sculptured candles are available everywhere in gorgeous shapes and various sizes and look fab whether they're brand new or half burned. Buy a bunch, arrange them around your pad—especially in the bathroom, an often-forgotten space that greatly benefits from added atmosphere—and light them up before the doorbell rings.

Scented candles have an intoxicating effect on even designated drivers. Unfortunately, the line between stinky and sultry is usually spelled out in the price tag. Skimp here and instead of creating a scented scene worthy of a grand mistress, you may end up with an aromatic ode to Grandma's house. Treat yourself to a luxury candle or two and light them often. Two of my favorites are Votivo, which go for around $12 and burn approximately thirty hours, and the far pricier, fabulously French-

FIRE AND WATER

For aquatic fun, float your tea lights—with or without their aluminum holders, which pop off with one tug of the wick. Find a glass bowl, a rocks glass (one candle per glass), or anything else transparent. Add drama to the bottom by dropping in something unusual that sinks and works well with the proportion of the container. I've combed the house and come up with cherries, which looked superb submerged, silverware, sand, rocks, marbles, colored dried beans, and jacks. If you don't have anything transparent for a container or want to go the rustic route, try a shallow wooden bowl or serving dish. Fill it with water and add something that floats such as flower petals, daisies, roses, sticks, or leaves. They not only look cool but also keep the tea lights from floating to the sides of the container. Place the tea lights where you want them in the water—either surrounded by other floating stuff or surrounding one centerpiece item such as a rose—and light them when the party starts. They won't burn completely because the water temperature stops the wax from melting down the sides, but they will light up your life for around two hours.

imported Diptyque, which cost close to $40 and burn about fifty hours (see the Resource Guide for details on both).

Add Flair with Flowers

Whether it's small statements or big bouquets, flowers add freshness to any room. If you have the time and the budget, add blossoms in any shape or size to every space. Put a single Gerber daisy in the bathroom, add an en-masse arrangement of calla lilies, tulips, or underrated everyday white daisies to the living room, snag a few wildflowers from the neighborhood for tiny tabletop vases, and create tight rose bouquets when bushes are in bloom. I'm a big fan of pussy willow branches because they're tall and dramatic, they have pretty puffs of fluff, and they last long after the party *and* your fresh flowers have died. When it comes to vases, use what you've got: float flowers in a bowl of water, jut them out of jam jars, or wrap them around champagne flute stems. Trick out the dinner table, too, but lay 'em low so they don't block the view.

Ready the Rest Room

A properly prepared bathroom is the sign of the most thoughtful and thorough hostess. But preparation is not merely about stocking up on toilet paper and making it self-serve in case you miss the replacement cue. Think of the bathroom as a mini-spa where guests can pamper, primp, *and* pee in style. Start with essentials: a pretty soap, clean hand towels, tissues, and toilet paper reserves somewhere obvious to anyone in need. Add aromatherapy with a scented candle and definitely a room spray. (Skip the cheesy canned stuff and get something tasteful from a perfume shop or specialty store.) Throw in a few flowers in a vase and you're good to go.

✳ Drinkin' and Smokin'

Make sure you pay attention to drink-friendly details. Whether you're anticipating calm waters with nonalcoholic beverages or battening down the hatches for a beer-and-wine blowout, distribute cocktail coasters or napkins around your pad so that your revelers have a proper place to drop their drinks. Also, don't forget to designate a smoking section that's armed with ashtrays. Even alleged nonsmokers come out of the clean-lung closet the minute there's a cocktail in hand and a cigarette in sight. If you permit puffing inside, set out plenty of ashtrays or tomorrow you'll be digging butts out of the plants and half-empty glasses. Likewise if you relegate smokers to the patio or your front steps.

✳ Tabletop Tricks

The tabletop is an entertaining area that can easily exude fabulousness and requires little more than a clever eye and a few five-minute arts-and-crafts projects. Plus, done with consideration for both form and function, it saves you from scampering to and from the kitchen once the fete's in full swing. No doubt it's a learned skill, but with a little practice even the novice party person can set a mean table.

The Sit-Down Meal

Sit-down meals are intimate, create an idyllic venue for people to talk to each other, and allow an opportunity to have some seriously fun table design. Set your scene for success by using your imagination and being creative with your tabletop accoutrements.

Only you know the depth of your collection of dishes, silverware, place mats, tablecloths, and chairs. Whatever you don't have won't be missed provided you set your table with a sense of humor and adventure. So what if you don't have salad forks or a complete set of silver, cups, and plates. Make your theme mix-and-match. If you're using paper plates and plastic forks or you don't have enough chairs to go around, spread out a blanket and some pillows and have an indoor picnic by candlelight. Haven't taken the tablecloth or place mat purchasing plunge? Get some butcher paper from your local grocery's meat section and include a centerpiece of crayons for an interactive artistic dinner—or draw place settings before your guests arrive. Add an element of surprise and thoughtfulness to your table and everything will work out wonderfully. In addition, consider the following tips:

- Unless you're offering bubbly and still options for water, fill water glasses beforehand (see the Fancy Water recipe in Chapter 10) and keep a pitcher on or near the table. Running for refills is no fun.

- Play with your silverware placement. Make an *X* over your napkins with a fork and knife. Wrap your utensils in napkins tied with ribbon, twine, or even chunky ponytail holders. Using chopsticks? Set them upright in a cup in the center of the table. A good table setting is not about whether the knife goes on the left or the right side. It's about creating a convivial space for gossip, gluttony, and an all-around good time.

◆ Work out the wineglass situation. Guests often get into the vino before they sit down to dine. So, use separate glasses for predinner drinks or expect to disrupt your table setting when corks get pulled.

◆ Have fun with place cards if you're feeling formal. Jordan Winery in Sonoma, California, hits its wine-country entertaining style home by writing its guests' names on corks. Martha Stewart's website suggests punching a hole in your paper name cards and tying them with twine or ribbon to the stems of pears, crab apples, and minipumpkins. When I was in a place-card pinch, I cased the house for last-minute potentials and spelled out the details with Scrabble pieces. Take a tour of your pad and search for fun ways to show guests where to sit. You can pen pals' names on bread plates with a squirt bottle filled with reduced balsamic vinegar (see Chapter 4) or melted chocolate. Or go with classic business-card-size name cards. Use thick paper and your best writing and prop them up in unusual ways—in between cherries or walnuts, dice, or Monopoly hotels. Write your guests' names on whatever you want with whatever you want. Just make it fun and consistent with the style of your table ensemble.

◆ Decorate. Once the essentials are in order, fill out the table with unobtrusive mood-enhancing knickknacks. Be bold, defy convention, make a statement, and get creative. Sprinkle an array of fall leaves, flower petals, or confetti. Add a few flower-filled vases or candles. If you're lacking cute candlesticks, fill a plate with a candle ensemble. At a loss for centerpiece decorations? Arrange branches, or curl some ribbon and stream it across the table or let it spill out of the wineglasses. Purchases are only part of a savvy party girl's repertoire. The rest is her ability to make something out of nothing—and pull it off with ample amusement and the greatest of ease.

The Buffet Table

When there are more mouths than there are seats or when you can't be bothered with clearing plates or serving seconds, the buffet table is a party girl's best friend. Once you've got the following bases covered and the party starts, you can let the self-service spread do all the work while you have all the fun. Keep in mind the following when setting up your buffet:

◆ Create a freestanding bar. Avoid a food-and-beverage bottleneck by placing the drink display on its own table away from the food. Guests are likely to make more return trips to the rum punch than the banana ice cream. Plus people tend to linger by the chips and dips. Stock the bar with all the essentials—extra glasses or plastic cups, cocktail napkins, ice, libations, mixers, and nonalcoholic options— and make refills easily accessible and self-serve. For details on luscious libation creations see Chapter 10.

◆ Make your food and beverage tables accessible from all sides if possible. A way to create a logjam at the lemonade stand is to stick a table in the corner where guests can access it from only one side. If you've got the room, make your service tables freestanding.

- Strategically organize your food display. Group napkins, plates, and silver (or plastic) together. Guests should be able to grab all their dining utensils without making a lap around the table. Always supply more of these than you think you'll need. Wandering diners almost always ditch their utensils and start anew with round two. Also arrange appetizers, mains, and desserts near each other.

- Supply a visible trash can. I used to play maid at all of my buffet parties. No longer. Now I put a trash can in plain view. When given the opportunity, most guests clean up after themselves. Likewise recycling bins, if you use them.

- Decorate around dishes. Going informal doesn't mean you should slack on the tabletop decor. Think of your buffet table as food-friendly art. Drape it with fabric. Decorate it with flowers, candles, potted plants, or anything else you have that's fun and that can fill in the holes.

Mood Music

Music is such a powerful mood-maker that you can instantly turn a romantic rendezvous into a roof-raising rager with a quick switch of the CD selection. The best hostesses double as DJs, but they rarely let their guests down with dead silence or a disappearing act to rifle through the CD collection. Conversely, they also know that turning the music down and the lights up is a polite way to tell guests it's time to get lost. Whenever you can, determine the preferred party vibe before guests arrive and make sure you're well stocked and ready to rock with your own favorites or some of the classics listed in the following sections, which will still be styling long after rapper Bow Wow can legally hit the bars. Organized by occasion, these must-haves are inoffensive to my conservative dad and jazz-singer mom but cool enough to appeal to my alternative-music-maven friends *and* the hip hottie of the month.

Breakfast of Champions

◆ *New Moon Daughter*, by Cassandra Wilson (Jazz). A voice as rich as molasses, a country-blues slant, and as soul-satisfying as warm milk with honey. Think toes in the grass, breakfast in bed, and romantic make-out sessions.

◆ *The Blues*, by Nina Simone (Blues). Modern legend Simone serves up the blues as they should be savored—with a deeply sultry and languid deliverance of longing, humanity, and suffrage.

◆ *Chez Moi*, by the Baguette Quartet (Retro Parisian Street Music). None of your friends will be one up on you with this French-inspired find. Start the morning with a retro romance of croissants and coffee and accordion-driven toe-tappers embodying Parisian music of the 1920s through 1950s.

The Lively Luncheon

◆ *Sister Bossa, Volume 2*, by various artists (Brazilian Jazz). Aptly self-described as "cool jazzy cuts with a Brazilian flavor," this modern take on classic Brazilian style is as happy as Snoopy when he's dancing and as sexy as tanned spaghetti-strapped shoulders. One of my all-time-favorite pool-party disks.

◆ *Buena Vista Social Club*, by Buena Vista Social Club (Cuban). The feel-good grooves of this celebrated Cuban band are lively and mellow, romantic and festive.

◆ *Black Ivory Soul*, by Angélique Kidjo (Afro-Latin Pop). Dave Matthews was wise to duet with this smooth-sailing young wonder whose African and Brazilian influences elevate the spirits and expectations of pop music.

◆ *Vhunze Moto*, by Oliver Mtukudzi (World Music). Broaden your breakfast or lunch offerings with the Zimbabwean riffs, happy-go-lucky percussions, and mesmerizing melodies by singer-composer Oliver Mtukudzi. Even if you can't speak his language, I promise you'll try to sing along.

Cocktail Classics

◆ *Songs for Swingin' Lovers!*, by Frank Sinatra (Jazz). When old blue eyes opens his mouth, you can almost taste the martinis.

◆ *The Genius of Ray Charles*, by Ray Charles (Jazz). Big band and ballads by one of jazz's true geniuses. Press play and slip into something comfortably chic.

◆ *Play*, by Moby (Techno). The brilliant bald boy's eclectic and soulful CD transcends techno with smooth grooves that go down easy and get you hooked.

- *Four Rooms*, The Original Motion Picture Soundtrack by Combustible Edison (Bachelor Pad Retro Pop). It was groovy long before Austin Powers, but to this CD he'd probably give the proverbial "Yeah, baby." Think *Breakfast at Tiffany's* on psychedelics.

- *Latin Groove*, by various artists/Putumayo World Music (Latin Dance). Take classic Cuban rhythms, add a dash of electronica and an arsenal of Latino talents, and stir up your inner Latin lover along with the cocktails.

- *The K&D Sessions*, by Kruder Dorfmeister (Acid Jazz/Trip–Ambient/Drum and Bass). An absolute must-have for the hip cocktail host, it's double pleasure with this dynamic two-CD set packed with way-cool remixes perfect for cocktail hour and chill time.

- *Tourist*, by St. Germaine (Acid Jazz). French composer-producer Ludovic Navarre creates jazzy electronic-music-inspired instrumentals ripe for playing even if you're not a techno fan.

Chillin'

- *Café del Mar, Volume 5*, compiled by José Padilla (Ambient/Trip-Hop). You can practically feel the breeze in your hair and waves lapping at your sandy toes with these mellow and carefree midtempo grooves. Even old folks feel welcome with this one.

- *Buddha Beats*, by various artists (Bouncy World Beat). These seductive, globally influenced songs could hypnotize even the most harried snake. Slip it on and kick it in the lotus position.

During Dinner

◆ *Kind of Blue*, by Miles Davis (Jazz). A mesmerizing collection of timeless tunes by one of jazz's greatest trumpeters. Start it at dinner and finish it in front of the fire.

◆ *The Best of the Songbooks*, by Ella Fitzgerald (Jazz). The consummate jazz singer sails through standards, setting a perfect dinnertime scene.

◆ *When I Look in Your Eyes*, by Diana Krall (Jazz). Today's jazz diva delivers standards with a finish that's as smooth, sweet, and upbeat romantic as *When Harry Met Sally*.

◆ *Free Fall*, by Jesse Cook (Rumba Flamenco). Passionate and sexy flamenco jams juice up the evening thanks to young and particularly tasty-looking guitarist Jesse Cook. The CD is perfect for barbecues and doubles as great road-trip music.

◆ *Joey DeFrancesco's Goodfellas*, featuring Joe Ascione and Frank Vignolia (Mafia Jazz). Break out the Chianti for Italian American–style instrumentals (such as "Fly Me to the Moon") led by killer organ licks and a Vegas lounge vibe. This one's definitely not in your friends' collections.

Old-Fashioned Romantic

◆ *Feeling Orange but Sometimes Blue*, by Ledisi (Jazz). A playful, soulful, and downright sultry CD and delicious dinner companion or accompaniment to a late-night glass of wine with someone you want to snuggle with. (If you can't find her locally, check out Amazon.com.)

◆ *Elaine Sings Jobim*, by Elaine Elias (Jazz). With a voice as smooth and seductive as Brazil's white-sand shores, Elias delivers bossa nova with an intimacy and elegance that can only amplify *amor*.

Straight-Up Seduction

◆ *Pure*, by The Golden Palominos (Elegantly Erotic). My friend's mom's boyfriend gave me this CD for my birthday with a side note that it was great for lovemaking. Though I thought it TMI (too much information), I've since conceded that he was right. There are no lullabies better for taking it seductively slow and lasciviously low.

Holiday Cheer

◆ *A Charlie Brown Christmas*, by Vince Guaraldi Trio (Jazz). Regardless of your religion, the original soundtrack from the TV special provides nostalgic Peanuts pleasures—especially when served with Peppermint Stick Martinis (see Chapter 10).

Get Your Groove On

Proper dance music depends on your taste. So, go with your own flow or play it safe with disco and funk classics, which allow everyone to raise the roof old-school style.

- *Disco Classics, Volume 1,* by various artists (Disco). PolyGram's disco disc covers the booty-shaking basics from Donna Summer, Kool & the Gang, and the Gap Band.

- *Millennium Hip-Hop Party,* by various artists (Hip-Hop). Bust a move with Young MC, set adrift on memory bliss with PM Dawn, jump around with House of Pain, and find out how it takes two to make a thing go right.

- *Millennium Funk Party,* by various artists (Funk). George Clinton, The Sugarhill Gang, and the Gap Band are among the funkmasters who will get your party peeps grinding.

- *Only Dance: 1975–1979,* by various artists (Disco). Break out your platforms and bell-bottoms for Earth, Wind & Fire, Chic, and Chaka Khan.

✳ Go For It

Now that you're armed with ideas on how to make your pad party friendly, one final tip: Be anything but bashful and predictable. Whether you drape your doorways in fabric or plastic beads, draw doodles on your bathroom mirror, serve breath-saving mints on a silver platter, custom create the perfect CD compilation, or serve McDonald's french fries in a crystal bowl, the way to make your pad stand out is to do things differently. Use your imagination, be fearless with the fun factor, and your food and beverages will taste that much better.

✳

IN MY EARLY twenties I shared an apartment with best friend, San Francisco–based artist Sarah Klein. Our combined annual salaries barely cracked $30,000, but our low-budget lifestyle and decor-impoverished pad didn't stop Sarah from turning functional items into decorative forms. She created installation art by arranging blue objects she found around the house, made pop art from stacked Campbell's soup cans, and adorned areas of the apartment with strategically placed books and found objects such as rocks and leaves. Twenty years later her tricks are still a simple way to transform ho-hum spaces into areas of interest. Turn a fresh eye onto your old stuff and you too can find whimsical ways to make everyday objects into works of art.

3

Painless
Party Planning

AT 3 A.M. ON the day of my thirtieth-birthday party, I knew I was crazy. In ten hours I would welcome fifty guests for an afternoon of mint juleps and seven different homemade finger foods, and after eighteen hours of cooking I was covered in chocolate praline pastry filling for a croquembouche and wondering whether caramelized sugar burns would scar. The event went well—even though Los Angeles traffic forced everyone to arrive two hours late—and my guests flipped for the food. But more important were the lessons I learned. Throwing a great party is not nearly as fun when you're too stressed and overworked to enjoy it. Besides, you know you're the tastiest morsel being served at your fete!

*

T he most crucial tactic for being a successful party girl is to ensure you have a blast at your own bash. Stress is never on the go-girl guest list, and it only crashes the party when the hurried hostess doesn't make a go-girl game plan or roll with the party-girl punches. In order to avoid pointless pitfalls, set yourself up for nearly effortless success with the guidelines in this chapter, which will help you wave away stress like a princess on parade.

✳ Preliminary Planning

Party planning can be as effortless as deciding to call a few friends and order a pizza, or more complicated with custom-created invites, a handful of homemade dishes, and specialty cocktails. Regardless of whether you've got ten minutes or ten days to prepare for your fiesta, it's important to make a winning game plan before you begin. To get you going, here are a few pointers:

◆ Determine how much time you want to spend on prep, and build your party around it. Just found out company's arriving in twenty minutes? Got an hour before the blowout? Planning an all-out feast next weekend? Review this chapter's list of Ready-Made Menus or browse the recipes and pick a strategy that works within your time frame. The less time you have to prepare, the less complicated your provisions should be. Whatever you do, keep it simple. Even effortless recipes become laborious when you're embarking on five of them at once.

- Don't overcommit. Build a menu of ready-made items and one or two easily prepared homemade highlights.

- Get a head count. Most *Last-Minute Party Girl* recipes are as easily multiplied as gremlins in water, but not without the provisions. Spread the party word with oral, Internet, or written invitations (see Chapter 1 for invitations information), tally your RSVPs, determine how many people you're expecting, and plan accordingly.

- Write out the menu, including drinks and any decorations. As your script for setting the scene, it will be invaluable when the curtain's about to rise and you've suddenly forgotten your lines. Tape it to the fridge, where it can't get buried under bread crumbs or tossed with the wet paper towels. Create concrete guidelines and, like that persistent drum-beating pink bunny, you'll be ever ready.

- Make a shopping list if you need to buy provisions. Check it twice. *Naughty* would be a kind way to describe the attitude of the usually nice hostess who has forgotten a critical item and has no time to look back. Don't forget to include nonfood and beverage needs such as napkins, toilet paper, ice, and candles.

- Shop as much in advance as possible. Whipping everything up at the last minute is far easier when you don't have to dash to the store, do your hair, and prepare the bread pudding in one stint.

- Consider enlisting a sous-chef (a.k.a. kitchen sidekick). An ambitious hostess often bites off more than she can chew, yet manages to keep her lipstick intact. How? She asks a friend to come over early and help. It not only keeps the atmosphere fun but also cuts the effort output in half.

♦ Give yourself more time than you think you'll need. Even as a veteran party girl, I foolishly allotted three and a half hours to prep a five-dish buffet feast for forty friends, including primp time and house, bar, and table setup. If it weren't for two extremely kind kitchen-savvy friends, I'd have wilted with the sautéed spinach. Make room for mishaps and bonbon breaks. No need to relinquish your princess posture when you put on the apron.

Midprep Mindfulness

The preparation that takes place after you've decided your menu and before your guests arrive is essential to a smooth ride once the party boat sets sail. Steer yourself toward the following directions, which help you stay on course as you cook, and even if the winds kick up, you'll be glamorously sailing through the gusts.

♦ Dress for success. Prepare and then primp, or the reverse. Either way, wear an apron, anticipate some spillage, and allot time for last-minute touch-ups. The comfortable party girl never tiptoes around the kitchen in fear of a flour-dusted fiasco and can even roll with a red wine stain when it finds its way to her new Michael Stars shirt. That said, every go-gal who's spent time in front of a hot stove benefits from a puff or two of powder before the doors swing open.

- Prepare your recipes in a logical order. Read through each of your recipes and get a sense of how your cooking flow should go. If a recipe requires a lot of chopping, marinating, cooking, or resting time, start it first. Easier items, like salad dressings and cheese plates, can be prepared during pauses. Also, guests like to participate. If you're going to play chef during prime party hour, assign easy tasks to willing guests. They're cheap labor and usually enthusiastic.

- Clean as you go. You're likely to use certain utensils, pots, and pans more than once during prep time, and you won't want to mine a mountain of dirty dishes to find them. Plus, the more the cookware and ingredients stack up, the less counter space you have.

- Don't get drunk—or at least, hold off on pulling the cork or sambaing with the cocktail shaker until you've got all your dining ducks in a row. Preparation pace and quality control usually get lost when libation intake gets lively. However, a glass of wine is definitely your friend when stress bubbles up with the pasta sauce.

- Rock out. There's no rule that says you can't pull your party prep off while getting your groove on to your favorite music. For optimum fun, shake it *and* bake it.

- Pace yourself. Even the most relaxed hostess has stressful moments. The thing that separates the party damned from the grande dame is what she does with it. Take a breathing break, blast the CD player and dance like a fool, call in kitchen reinforcements, or just take a moment to remind yourself it's all in the name of fun.

◆ Don't sweat it. The best parties I've attended had more to do with the company and the spirit than perfection of penne. Serve up your sincere and sassy energy on a silver platter, focus on quality time with your guests rather than the evening's imperfections, and no matter what you serve, the party will be memorable.

✳ Ready-Made Menus

When I begin planning a party, I often dig through dozens of magazines to piece together recipes that suit my occasion, schedule, budget, and intended style. But if you're looking for menu guidance, you don't need to flip through pages to figure out which side dish to serve with the sautéed salmon. These Ready-Made Menus tell you how to be fast and fabulous during an entertaining emergency, what to whip up when you have two hours or less, how to take it over the top, and wonderful ways to get by on the cheap.

Dig in, and don't forget: (1) ask guests to bring a beverage, and (2) don't make everything from scratch. Getting guests to bear some of the financial burden and adding quality store-bought items to your home-made extravaganza are the secrets to every sane party girl.

The Cocktail Party

Go practical and glamorous. Set up a self-serve station for snacks and drinks, including napkins, glasses, and appetizer plates. Make provisions based on your head count—and keep refills tucked away in the kitchen.

EMERGENCY When you've got about ten minutes to prep before the party people stampede your scene, turn to your Party Girl Pantry provisions. (For a complete list and more detailed information, see Chapter 4.) Break out crackers, fan them across a platter, and finish them with a ready-made spread. Display cheeses surrounded by grapes and sliced pears, figs, and a sliced French baguette with an olive-oil dipping sauce. Stand breadsticks in a glass. Drain your roasted bell peppers and put them in a pretty bowl. Slice some salami. Crack open a bag of tortilla chips and a jar of salsa. Toss olives in a bowl, accompanied by a bowl for pits. Any combo of the preceding will do. For larger parties, fill lots of tummies with Crudités (Chapter 5), or slice up a red bell pepper and a few celery sticks and arrange them with baby carrots. Stick 'em next to bought hummus or classic onion dip (sour cream mixed with packaged onion soup mix). If you've got five minutes to spare, add a homemade touch with Elegant Endives or Suzanne Goin's Parmesan-Stuffed Dates (both in Chapter 5). Serve a specialty cocktail from Chapter 10, round it out with beer and non-alcoholic selections, light a few candles, and take a breath. Now don your tiara, press play on your favorite CD, and strike a sassy pose.

TWO HOURS OR LESS Pick your favorites from the preceding Emergency instructions and add to them Bite-Size Bumstead Sandwiches, Quesadillas, Bruschetta, or sliced and sautéed sausages with a mélange of mustards as well as Lucques Olives and Almonds (all in Chapter 5). Other homemade options you can mix and match with Party Girl Pantry items include Guacamole (Chapter 5) and chips, which says olé when served with Maui Margaritas (Chapter 10) and Party Girl Pizza (Chapter 5), which takes just over two hours but requires little face time with the food and will astound your guests. Or make a double batch of The Jimtown Store's Fig and Black Olive Tapenade (Chapter 5), hide half for your next fete, and watch your guests freak with newfound fondness for you. If time's on your side, scour the house for extra decorative touches to add to your cocktails spread. Throw flowers in vases, pick out your music selections, light a scented candle in the bathroom, slip into something slinky, christen the cocktail station, and toast yourself.

OVER THE TOP It's all about luxury, so whatever beverage you serve, make it in martini glasses or champagne flutes. Then seduce with your choice of appetizers from Chapter 5, such as velvety Salmon Rillettes, buttery Warm Brandade Gratin, or store-bought pâté with Tiny Toasts. Add an adventurous cheese selection (see Chapter 4) on a tray or cutting board graced with grapes, sliced pears or apples, fresh figs, or Caramelized Nuts. Fill a big tray with Crudités surrounding a centerpiece bowl of Tarragon Dip or store-bought spread. Add Oysters in the Raw or Wolfgang Puck's Smoked Salmon and Caviar on Buckwheat Cakes and you're instantly legendary among your friends. See Chapter 5 for recipes.

ON THE CHEAP Forget fancy cheeses and pâtes. Go straight for Bruschetta or Quesadillas, Crudités, and sliced pita bread triangles served with Aimee's Hummus (all in Chapter 5). Make Sangria or buy a big bottle of generic vodka and cruise the other selections in Chapter 10, "Liquid Pleasures," to determine your house specialty drink. Ask guests to bring a bottle of wine, a six-pack of brewskies, or nonalcoholic beverages.

Romantic Dinner (doubles as an elegant dinner for 4 to 8)

Whether you're romancing your new beau or your best friends, nothing seduces like the following dinner menus, which are as glamorous in looks as they are in flavor. Don't forget to offer coffee with dessert.

EMERGENCY No matter what you serve, start with bubbly—and stay with it straight through after-dinner couch athletics if you like. If you've got a good seafood purveyor nearby, flavor-burst your bubbles with store-shucked Oysters in the Raw, or keep it simple with Elegant Endives (both in Chapter 5). Make your first course a Tip of the Iceberg Salad (Chapter 6) with store-bought blue cheese dressing, or a simple mixed green salad and avocado slices tossed in olive oil and a touch of balsamic vinegar and salt. During summer you can also turn to tomatoes for a Caprese Salad (Chapter 6). Follow up with a fabulously fast pasta dish made with Hiro's Heroic Tomato Sauce or Angel Hair Pasta with Smoked Salmon and Golden Caviar (both in Chapter 7). Don't forget to start the water boiling long before you need it. Magnify the evening's mojo with hand-fed Strawberries and Sweet Cream, or ice cream with Homemade Caramel Sauce (both in Chapter 9), chocolate chips, and chopped store-bought toffee. Stick with slow grooves or jazz standards through the evening, and keep food portions moderate. Smooching and snuggling aren't nearly as fun when you're trying to suck in a bloated belly.

TWO HOURS OR LESS Give your man a stiff one (a drink, that is). Likewise yourself. Have a small snack on hand—think cheese (Chapter 4), Crudités and dip, or Bruschetta (both Chapter 5). If he's not too much of a meat-and-potatoes man, freshen up your piqued palates with Apple, Endive, and Stilton Salad (Chapter 6). Otherwise, play it safe with mixed greens embellished with a simple dressing and your favorite toppings (see "Glamorize Your Greens" in Chapter 6). You won't be fishing for compliments, but you'll definitely get them if you serve broiled fish marinated in Hiro's Mother Sauce or Two-Second Teriyaki-Style Salmon (both in Chapter 7), which incite infatuation when served with Haricots Verts and Rice (both in Chapter 8). Likewise the meatier option of Painless Pan-Fried Steak with Red Wine Sauce (Chapter 7) accompanied by Potatoes with Parsley (Chapter 8). (If you're serving eight, forget about steak. It's expensive, and you'll end up in front of the stove too long.) Want to skip the sides and stay vivacious and vegetarian? Turn to Fettuccine with Swiss Chard, Currants, Walnuts, and Brown Butter (Chapter 7). Dessert? Aside from your sweet lips, Chocolate-Dipped Desires (Chapter 9) woo the wanton male. Pour lots of wine during dinner. It whets the appetite. Note: If you're going with fish, don't forget to marinate it before you do anything else—it's the most time-sensitive part of party prep.

OVER THE TOP Do it Donna Summer–style: Dim all the lights, sweet darling, 'cuz tonight it's all the way. When it comes to seductive starters, nothing beats *caviahhh*, darlink. Unless it's more caviar—and chilled shots of vodka, martinis, or sparkling wine (see Chapters 4 and 10). More affordable appetizers *de amore* are Flying Fish Grill Pan-Fried Oysters, Oysters in the Raw, and Wolfgang Puck's Smoked Salmon and Caviar on Buckwheat Cakes (all in Chapter 5). Serve them before seating your guest (or guests). Keep the wine flowing, and kick off dinner with show-stopping starters such as Sautéed Diver Scallops with Cauliflower, Capers, and

Almonds (Chapter 5), Roasted Beet and Fennel Salad, or Jean-Paul Picot's Gratinéed Onion Soup (both in Chapter 6). Then secure your goddess status by serving up Sautéed Quail (or Chicken) with Roasted Red Onion Panzanella (Chapter 7). Make the finale grand with Puff Daddies or Chocolate Toffee Crunch Cakes (both in Chapter 9).

ON THE CHEAP Open a bottle of inexpensive sparkling wine and mix it with a fruit juice or a liqueur for fancy flare (see Chapter 10 for suggestions). Hand-feed your friend Lucques Olives and Almonds (Chapter 5) before sauntering to the table to serve Tip of the Iceberg Salad with Blue Cheese Dressing, Mom's House Salad, or Butternut Squash Soup (all in Chapter 6). If you're serving two to four people, get wholesome with rustically romantic Whole Roasted Chicken and Roasted Vegetables (Chapter 7). For larger parties make a double batch of Sue's Italian Chicken Stew (Chapter 7) served with yellow rice or Polenta (Chapter 8). Freak your friends, lovers, or both with gorgeous servings of Coffee Granita (Chapter 9), which are sure to keep everyone lively for after-dinner follies.

Twenty-Person Buffet Feast

Have myriad mouths to feed? No worries. Mind these menus to easily offer an outrageous spread. Multiply the recipes to heed your head count, and remember that each dish doesn't need to feed twenty people, provided you have a few options. The greater the selection, the more your guests will nibble through the meal on smaller portions. Also, it's a good idea to ask some of your more food-savvy party friends to ante up with additional snacks, side dishes, or desserts. At the very least, invite everyone on your guest list to bring wine, beer, or other beverages.

EMERGENCY If you're brave enough to invite twenty people over to eat at the very last minute, you are definitely the kind of person who can handle putting it together with panache. Mix up a mean pitcher of Maui Margaritas (Chapter 10). Display snacks—tortilla chips and a store-bought salsa (get more salsa than you think you'll need), cheeses (Chapter 4), sweet French baguette slices, and fresh fruits cut into chunks and mixed in a serving bowl. No one has high expectations for last-minute feasts, so don't even attempt to make half the provisions from scratch. Order pizza and serve it with a huge bowl of Mom's House Salad with sliced tomatoes and avocados or Caprese Salad (both in Chapter 6). Or go for Chinese food or any other inexpensive takeout that will keep you out of the kitchen. When dessert is due, whip up Homemade Caramel Sauce (Chapter 9) and serve it with ice cream and self-serve bowls of chocolate chips and chopped toffee. Or purchase ready-to-bake cookie dough (available in grocery stores) and pop it in the oven. No one can resist freshly baked cookies.

TWO HOURS OR LESS Start Godfathers (Chapter 5) from scratch because they require the most time. Don't forget to multiply the recipes to meet your head count. Fill your food table with Crudités and Aimee's Hummus (both in Chapter 5) or a store-bought dip. Double the recipe for Apple, Endive, and Stilton Salad or Caesar Salad (both in Chapter 6). Follow the Chicken Roulades recipe (Chapter 7), only serve the thighs whole rather than cut into wheels, and add Oven-Roasted Vegetable Skewers (Chapter 8). If your party's in spring or summer, keep dessert bright and light in the form of Pineapple with Fiery Sugar Dip (Chapter 9). To satisfy the more serious sweet tooth, triple the recipe for Strawberry and Rhubarb Cobbler (Chapter 9), which can cook while you and your guests enjoy your meal. (Set a timer and keep it near you, so you remember to take the treat out of the oven.) Don't forget to make the bar easily accessible and self-serve.

OVER THE TOP First thing in the morning, start a triple batch of Slow-Cooked Beef Stew (Chapter 7). When you're close to party time, prepare the partnering Polenta or Mashed Potatoes (both in Chapter 8). Get a huge tray or cutting board and create a cornucopia of pop-in-your-mouth ready-made foods fit for the gods. Think a variety of cheeses and crackers (Chapter 4), Tiny Toasts (Chapter 5) or sliced French baguette, The Jimtown Store's Fig and Black Olive Tapenade (Chapter 5) or any sexy ready-made spread, salami, cantaloupe wrapped in prosciutto, grapes, figs (when in season), Whole Roasted Garlic (Chapter 5), and Lucques Olives and Almonds (Chapter 5) or mixed nuts. Double the recipe for Deep-Dish Cobb Salad or any salad of your choice (see Chapter 6). Pull out the stops and go for Bread Pudding with Bourbon Sauce or Double-Chocolate Biscotti (both in Chapter 9) and ice cream.

ON THE CHEAP Stick with a one-drink theme, but still request that everyone bring a beverage. (See Chapter 10 for drink suggestions.) Load up on Crudités and Aimee's Hummus (both in Chapter 5). Make a huge serving bowl of Roasted Red Onion Panzanella (the bread salad portion from the Sautéed Quail with Roasted Red Onion Panzanella recipe) and serve it with Chicken Roulades (both in Chapter 7), which are extremely cheap and can be made en masse on a large baking sheet. If it's an evening fete, add a side of Potato Gratin or Couscous (both in Chapter 8). Finish with the ever spectacular and racy red Strawberry and Rhubarb Cobbler (Chapter 9).

✳ Thoughts on Themes

While mulling over your menu, consider your event's theme and determine whether you can amplify the fun factor by adding effortless amusements or asking attendees to participate. The following ideas have all made it onto my itinerary.

Brunch

Whether it's a bridal or baby shower or a morning blowout among gal pals, there's an easy and elegant way to feed your favorite chowhounds. Simply start by preparing Quiche Lorraine (Chapter 7), add any salad (see Chapter 6) and a bowl of chopped fruit (think strawberries, cantaloupe, bananas, oranges, apples, and whole grapes and blueberries), and throw in a basket of store-bought bakery items such as croissants, banana bread, or muffins with butter and jam, or stock up on bagels, cream cheese, lox, red onions, and capers. Keep the sparkling wine flowing and you're all good.

Birthday Bash

For birthday parties I don't like to act my age. I go for goofy paper hats, playing pin the tail on the donkey, and topping my cake with chunky number-shaped candles. You can liven up your soiree with sparklers, sparkling candles, childhood games, or balloons, or make Chocolate Toffee Crunch Cakes (Chapter 9) and get guests to frost and decorate their own. Another classic? A tiara for the birthday babe, of course.

Finger Foods

When it's cocktail party time and I don't want to deal with cutlery chaos, I serve nothing but finger foods accompanied by plenty of plates and napkins. If you want to play with your food, serve any of the following (see Chapter 5 for recipes): Crudités along with breads, spreads, dips, and cheeses, Bruschetta, Lucques Olives and Almonds, Quesadillas, Bite-Size Bumstead Sandwiches, Oysters in the Raw, Flying Fish Grill Pan-Fried Oysters, Party Girl Pizza, or Godfathers.

Barbecues

Talk about a great way to stealthily transfer the burden to your guests. Tell everyone to bring his or her own meat and a beverage, load up on charcoal, make sides such as salad, easy appetizers, and dessert, and when the party boys arrive, watch them work the barbecue like hired hands.

Puppet Party

Costume parties can be too much pressure for perennially busy perfectionist go-girls and guys. Instead, ask your guests to don a hand or finger puppet. Have a few extras around for those who forget to arrive with an alter ego. It may sound ridiculous, but you'd be amazed at how quick people are to play when given the chance.

White Trash

Slumming it can be sexy, especially when it's intentional and well executed. One of the best parties at *Food & Wine* magazine's annual Classic at Aspen was a private late-night rager thrown by perpetual party girl and

New York–based food writer and editor Kate Krader, who wanted people to have fun with their food. The menu? "White trash" foods and lots of libations. Guests such as chefs Mario Batali, Emeril Lagasse, and Bobby Flay and most of the magazine's editorial staff crowded a funky retro condo for pizza pockets, a Velveeta sculpture contest, and bottomless bowls of M&Ms. If you're going to go for kitsch food, take it all the way: Use single-wrapped American cheese as coasters. Serve ice-cream sandwiches made with Pop-Tarts. Pass Jell-O shooters (frozen Jell-O made with vodka, for those of you who missed the frat parties). Definitely don't forget the spray cans of cheese and some crackers. Basically, have fun with it. Serve up the party spirit and your guests can't help but have a good time. (A few strong cocktails don't hurt either.)

*

WHEN I WAS in my twenties, I was out on the town in San Francisco. I'd just finished dining at Haight Ashbury's very happening Cha Cha Cha and scooped up the token Tootsie Rolls that arrive with the check. My roommate and partner in crime Sarah The Artist and I headed to Julie's Supper Club, a funky bar where we were promptly harassed by a lovelorn barfly. A chivalrous hunk of a human kindly came to the rescue, elbowing in on our wanna-be suitor. To express my gratitude, I reached into my pocket and rewarded him with a Tootsie Roll. He was surprisingly pleased. Our next stop was an upscale singles bar where everyone stoically sipped and no one was having fun. We pulled out a Tootsie Roll and asked what people would do to win a piece of our enticing chewy candy. We got male belly dances, tongue tricks, and instant karaoke.

When it was time to pay for our chardonnays, the bartender charged us two Tootsie Rolls and sent us on our way. We knew we were on to something.

The next weekend we had no sweets in our pockets but wanted to bar-hop armed with party favors. We scoured the house, but all we could find was single-wrapped slices of American cheese. It was not exactly what we had in mind, but with no alternative, we popped the orange slabs into our purses and headed to our favorite San Francisco dance club. When we tried to pay our admission with our processed prizes, the doorman wanted none of it, but inside we bought drinks with cheese, threw it down on the dance floor and gyrated around it like pagans, and even peeled off the wrapper and placed a cheese square in the center of a reveler's shiny bald head. After we'd tried on three subsequent occasions with the stone-faced doorman, even he finally succumbed to the power of the cheese. Since then I've hit the hottest Hollywood dance floors with a pint-size Pillsbury Doughboy as my dance partner, peeked finger puppets out from under the table at the most refined restaurants, and broken out in song during the sorbet course. If there's one thing I've learned as a party girl, it's that there is always room for the absurd. In fact, the more absurdity you can bring to the party, the more fun you'll have. All people need is a little encouragement to be playful and they're quick to jump into the sandbox. As the party girl, it's your job to bring the shovel and the pail.

4

The Party Girl Pantry

THINGS DON'T ALWAYS go right with recipes, but the party girl never lets kitchen catastrophes spoil a meal. I can point to occasions when I had to swallow my pride with the overcooked pork or grin and bear my oversalted Thai salad. I've taken a fire extinguisher to a chicken flaming in my oven and stunk up the house with burned salmon that I forgot under the broiler. I also had my *San Francisco Magazine* editor seated at the dinner table when I reached into the oven with a damp oven mitt to grab $40 worth of my favorite broiled fish, and the Pyrex baking dish shattered like safety glass. (It's worth noting that Pyrex is not designed to go under the broiler or directly onto open flames.) Only after prepping for Wolfgang Puck's incredible Meals on Wheels fundraiser for two days in a kitchen with more than a dozen of the nation's top chefs did I see that even the world's most prestigious food folks have kitchen calamities, routinely burn things, and work around blunders. It's all part of the cooking experience. So, when the shiitake hits the fan, don't distress: pull out your pantry items and whip up an easy pasta, order a pizza, or ask your guests if

they're up for adventure dining. Ultimately the party is about the people, not what's on the plate.

✳

sually I plan in advance for entertaining, but it's not uncommon that guests are twenty minutes away and I haven't combed my hair, let alone figured out what to feed my friends. Enter the Party Girl Pantry, my list of must-haves that allow me to create a gorgeous spread with little more than a crank of the can opener and twist of a jar top. My cupboards aren't overflowing with everything on the party pantry list, but with even a fraction of these essentials I can whip up a full-blown fiesta of appetizers and cocktails in fifteen minutes flat. (An actual dinner usually requires a few additional ingredients and a little more time.) Make a habit of tossing one or two of these survival supplies into your basket whenever you cruise the aisles of the grocery store and before you know it, your pantry will be party ready.

Think of the Party Girl Pantry as a starter kit for entertaining. It'll familiarize you with kitchen essentials, give you ideas for last-minute appetizers, and partner with recipes and menu themes in this book. For your party-girl pleasure it's divided into four categories. Basic Entertaining Equipment is all the kitchen hardware you'll need to get the party started. Ever-Ready Items are essentials you can tuck away on a shelf and forget about until you need them. They pair with Party Girl Perishables— or fresh fare that won't last for months. Bar Keeps comprise bartending basics and essentials. Combined in whole or in part in your cupboard, the pantry items are everything you'll need so that during entertaining emergencies—when you don't have time to shop and cook—your home will still be a most gracious haven.

✳ Basic Entertaining Equipment

Beyond basic utensils like plates, silverware, pots, and pans, having a few other essentials will help ensure that the hurried hostess produces her party with nary a nibble to her freshly manicured nails. Stock your kitchen with the basics, and the party can practically start without you.

BLENDER It's wicked for whipping up smoothies, blender drinks, purees, and soups.

BASIC ENTERTAINING EQUIPMENT

Blender	Corkscrew	Measuring cups
Bottle opener	Cutting board	Measuring spoons
Can opener	Film	Pitcher
Ceramic ramekins	Food processor	Serving bowls
Champagne flutes	Garlic press	Serving platters
Cocktail shaker	Knives	Serving utensils
Coffee grinder	Mandoline	Timer
Coffeemaker	Martini glasses	Wineglasses

BOTTLE OPENER Only fools with great dental insurance and little common sense admit to having successfully opened a beer bottle with their teeth. (Seriously, don't try this at home.) A more civilized last-ditch alternative is a key (pry up the sides bit by bit). But for god's sake, there's no logical reason why you can't spring for an opener. (See "Can opener" for the combo package.)

CAN OPENER No doubt you already have one—especially if you lived in college dorms. If you're the one person on the planet who hasn't invested in one or realized how critical it is, try opening a can without one. A bonus: Many come with a bottle opener.

CERAMIC RAMEKINS These white oven-safe containers are frivolities for sure, but in single-serving sizes they also make special occasions out of otherwise basic side dishes and desserts. They're also great for filling with dips, olives, and anything else that should be served in a cute and very small container. Buy six or more ramekins—three and a half inches in diameter—from any culinary shop. (See the Resource Guide for sources.)

CHAMPAGNE FLUTES Not an imperative purchase, but truth is that drinking bubbly out of any other type of glass isn't nearly as glamorous. If you've got the extra bank and shelf space, go for it. FYI, the preferred shape for a sparkling wine glass is the elongated "flute." Its length allows steady streams of bubbles—or the "bead"—to beautifully wind their way to the surface. Its shape also better pronounces the wine's "bouquet," or aromas, and keeps the wine cooler longer than the wider, flatter, saucer-shaped sparkling wine glasses. Besides, they look *mahvalous.*

COCKTAIL SHAKER If you're into martinis, you've got to commit. Using McGuyver maneuvers in the kitchen is one thing, but it's hard to look cool and shake cocktails in Tupperware.

COFFEE GRINDER Freshly ground coffee is worlds better than grinds that have grown old in the freezer. Plus, this affordable gadget does double duty as a nut grinder.

COFFEEMAKER Until Starbucks delivers, even the laziest of party girls must invest in a coffeemaker. Besides, it's amazing how much respect you can garner from making a good cup of coffee (i.e., strong, so go heavy on the grinds). For added flair, brew up an old-world vibe with a French press.

CORKSCREW You can't open a bottle of wine without one, unless, of course, it's a screw top. There are dozens of styles of corkscrews on the market. The prettier, the pricier, but more important is knowing the four main types that can pop your wine-stop. Easiest on the novice is the "wing corkscrew"; screw it in and the arms go up, push the arms down and the cork comes out. Lose the wings and add extra money and technology, and you've got "power corkscrews," which, like most other power tools, take the manual out of the labor—only these don't require batteries or a plug, and the lever does all the work for you. A "waiter's corkscrew" is the basic sort that folds into itself like a pocketknife and has a screw, a small knife, and a hinged handle. Finally, there's the "Ah So" cork puller, which is preferred by serious winos, since it keeps the cork intact when you wedge its two prongs into the bottle between the cork and the glass and pull out the cork with a twist of its handle. The best corkscrew for you is a matter of personal preference, but buy one of quality. I've had the spiral section of a cheap waiter's-style wine opener break in half in my cork. Talk about getting screwed.

CUTTING BOARD There's no getting around it. Even if you're in an apartment, you won't want to slash your countertops. Buy a good-size board—wood or plastic.

FILM Evidence is essential to the party girl. Whether your motivation is to stock the scrapbook, document the dramas, or blackmail friends, make sure your camera is always fully loaded. I also have a few instant cameras around for when we're playing too hard to let the quality camera partake.

FOOD PROCESSOR An essential for the last-minute cook, this miracle contraption slices, minces, mixes, shreds, and cuts hours off your prep time. If you don't have one and plan on cooking with any regularity, buy one.

GARLIC PRESS There's no easy way to get the same mashed-garlic results without it. Good-quality presses are hard to come by but worth seeking. Find one that's sturdy, made of metal, and all in one piece.

KNIVES Splurge on high-quality knives. Seriously. Cooking is harder and more time consuming without them. Get the basics: a paring knife (small, nimble), bread knife (medium-size, serrated), and chef knife (at least eight inches, not serrated, and well balanced in your hand). Comfortable knives are a matter of personal preference. Hold them and make sure they feel good in your hand before you commit. (Likewise your man.)

MANDOLINE Only the extremely detailed party girl need invest in this fancy cutting contraption that simplifies slicing foods into styles such as french fry, matchstick, diced, waffle, and ultrathin. But if supercool shapes and paper-thin slices are part of your entertaining plan, it's a wise investment. They can cost more than $100, but I bought a decent mandoline by Benriner for $30 via the Internet.

MARTINI GLASSES They turn a basic cocktail into a Frank Sinatra scene, they're just that cool. If you've got 'em, flaunt 'em. If you want a collection without paying the price, see the "How" section under "Inspiring Invitations" in Chapter 1.

MEASURING CUPS A kitchen essential. If you don't already have one, be sure to get a good set or a clear Plexiglas cup with multiple measurement demarcations.

MEASURING SPOONS Following recipe instructions is hard enough without throwing a measurement guessing game into the mix. These are essential for keeping the party fare properly seasoned.

PITCHER You can get by without one, but it'll save you lots of legwork when concocting a burly batch of margaritas or refilling water glasses during dinner.

SERVING BOWLS The more, the merrier, but you should have at least three—one in a cheery country pattern for daytime, another in a sleek Asian design for night, and a basic white one for anytime. They're crucial for salads and pastas. (See the Resource Guide for sources.)

SERVING PLATTERS If you haven't already, pick up a few gorgeous platters. You're nowhere in the party-hosting world without something stunning to show off your culinary prowess. (See the Resource Guide for sources.)

SERVING UTENSILS They seem so trivial until it's time to serve the salad or pasta and you're stuck with soupspoons. Get two pairs at least. Designer tongs are good, too. Trust me. You'll need 'em and you can never have enough.

TIMER If your oven doesn't have one built in, don't even think about skipping out on this critical instrument. When guests show up early and you're applying eyeliner with one hand and whisking with the other, a timer's ding can be the difference between a fantastic homemade meal and a panicked dial-up to Domino's.

WINEGLASSES They are far better for swirling and sniffing than jam jars and look great on the table. Start with a basic style that will do the trick for red or white. Stay away from extremely thin stems—they'll snap soon and you'll be right back at the store racking up charges on your credit card. My very fun friend master sommelier Evan Goldstein says, "The bigger the glass, the bigger the party." Hear, hear.

Ever-Ready Items

These are the calming cornerstones to any perennial party girl because they can be bought well in advance and won't spoil until leg warmers are back in style (well, almost that long).

BALSAMIC VINEGAR The world's undisputed champion of vinegars, balsamic is made in Italy from Trebbiano grapes. It gets its dark, rich, and tangy-sweet character through aging in a number of wood barrels that decrease in size (and increase in vinegar-wood contact) as the liquid ages, evaporates, and condenses. The longer it ages, the better, more intensely flavored, and more expensive it is. I've never bought vinegar that cost more than $20 per bottle—and even throwing down more than $10 puts a lump in my budget-minded throat. But when it comes to balsamic, you really do get what you pay for, so it's worth turning your nose up at the proverbial bottom-of-the-barrel varieties. Besides, it will last you through many parties. Use it for superb salad dressings and marinades, add it to

EVER-READY ITEMS

Balsamic vinegar	Napkins	Sodas and sparkling
Breadsticks	Nuts	water
Candles	Olive oil (extra-virgin)	Spreads
Chocolate	Olives	Sugar and spice
Coffee	Pasta	Sun-dried tomatoes
Crackers	Peperoncinis	Tapenade
Edamame	Pita	Tea
Frozen foods	Puff pastry dough	Tomato sauce
Ibuprofen	Roasted red peppers	Toothpicks
Ice	Salami	Tortilla chips
Ice cream	Salsa	
Mints	Sausages	

olive oil for a fast bread dip, or boil it down to a "balsamic reduction" (a few minutes on the stove until it's thick) and drizzle it on baked stone fruits such as nectarines and peaches. Reducing balsamic vinegar intensifies the flavors and thickens the liquid into rich, sexy syrup perfect for drizzling on fruit, ice cream, dinner plates, or anything else that will benefit from some tantalizing tang.

BREADSTICKS They're sleek, stylishly shaped, and perfect for scooping up tasty spreads and dips. Plus, unopened they'll stay crisp until you need them. I set them upright in a vase or jar to add an architectural element to my snack tray.

CANDLES Their warm glow and flickering flame make every evening sexier. But even during daytime parties I set the scene with a scented candle, which spreads seductive aromas through my living room and bathroom. Build a collection of tea lights, dripless tapers, at least one set of candlesticks if you don't have any, and scented and sculpturally shaped varieties. Check out Chapter 2 for tips on how to make them light up your party life.

CHOCOLATE There's no such thing as too much chocolate. You can bake with it, take a vegetable peeler to it and sprinkle it over dessert, dip foods and fingers in it when it's melted, make hot chocolate and mochas, and swallow a few nibbles while cooking just because you feel like it. I've got truffles at my makeshift bar; Nestle's and See's chocolate chips in the freezer; Scharffen Berger semisweet and bittersweet chocolate blocks in a drawer; and cocoa nibs (toasted cocoa beans), Ibarra Mexican chocolate, and various cocoa powders on my kitchen shelf. Fortunately, my emotional eating errs on the savory side, so I rarely pilfer in between parties. If you can hang with chocolate in the house, stock up. Otherwise, pick it up at the last minute and your finales will always be bittersweet in the best possible sense.

COFFEE I'm not sure which is worse, bad coffee or no coffee. Make sure you're well supplied with the good stuff—fresh-roasted, turbo-charged, heart-rate-jumping java. (Ideally in whole beans, provided you have a grinder.) Keep it in the freezer and pull it out to accompany dessert, perk up designated drivers, or make your kitchen smell seductive for that unexpected breakfast guest. (You know what I'm talking about.) Don't forget decaf. Trust me: the greater the number of guests over thirty years of age, the higher the ratio of no-caffeine requests.

CRACKERS Properly packaged and stored, they're crunchy, versatile, and godsends in a party-girl pinch. Have at least two types on hand—Carr's water crackers are nationally distributed safe bets. But better yet are locally produced crackers, which I can usually find if I snoop around in a gourmet grocer. When instant appetizers are in order, fan your crackers out on a plate or stick them in a basket and serve them with edible accoutrements such as cheese, pâte, and finger-food-friendly fruits or veggies such as grapes, cherries, cucumber or celery sticks, or baby carrots.

EDAMAME These fresh soybeans often served in Japanese restaurants come frozen, are good to go after a few minutes in boiling water, and, once salted and served, are fun to slide through your teeth, forcing the beans to pop out of their pods. In recent years they've become popular enough that you can usually find them in gourmet groceries or, if all else fails, in Asian supermarkets. Put them in a blue bowl that offsets their green color and provide an extra bowl for ditching the empty pods.

FROZEN FOODS If you serve ready-made appetizers like miniquiches and pot stickers, mingle them with freshly made items such as vegetables, dips, cheeses, breads, and unique spreads that are not members of the stereotypical cocktail spread society. The point of the entertaining go-girl is to make every party morsel her own. These pervasive snacks have made so many cocktail appearances that they're the character actors of the everyday buffet. Give them a supporting role, not star status.

IBUPROFEN OK, so maybe it should be in the bathroom cabinet, but if you party with the vigor of most go-girls, you'll need this headache helper close at hand. Go for the generic labels rather than pointlessly paying name brands' jacked-up prices.

ICE Even the hottest party can run cold if there's not enough ice to keep the rocks glasses clinking. But it's tough stocking up in advance, since bags of ice become blocks if they hang around too long in the freezer, and tray cubes get half disintegrated and downright funky in a few weeks. Make sure your ice trays are freshly filled, and stock up on a few bags a day or two before party time.

ICE CREAM I know. Keeping ice cream around is a lot to ask. But if it's in the freezer, you need only add toppings—chocolate sauce, candied nuts, reduced balsamic, espresso, baked fruit, or anything your hostess heart desires—and you've got a decadent dessert. When it comes to ice cream, quality is key, so always buy the good stuff—like Häagen-Dazs or

Ben & Jerry's. Vanilla is the best flavor for flexibility, since it goes well with almost everything and is neutral enough to please various palates. Can't resist temptation? Forget it. You'll just have to dash to the store when ice cream is part of the dessert deal. And don't forget bonbons. The name alone epitomizes luxury and leisure.

MINTS Even if the evening calls for nothing but air kisses, it's always good to have breath mints displayed on the cocktail table, distributed during the party, or passed when guests are heading out the door. Expert go-girls don't let friends stink and drive.

NAPKINS Even the elementary hostess knows the necessity of the napkin. What she may not know is that she's run out. Check your stock. Make sure you have good-quality dinner and cocktail napkins. Otherwise, it could get ugly.

NUTS So easy with such great rewards, toasted or candied walnuts, pecans, almonds, or pine nuts add flavor and crunch to salads, pastas, and even desserts. Buy 'em raw—and in bulk because they're much cheaper than those foolishly priced airtight packages—roast them (see the Toasted Nuts recipe in Chapter 5), and throw them on whatever you want for last-minute pizzazz. Store-bought mixed nuts are also great in a pinch when put in a pretty container and placed in the center of the action.

OLIVE OIL (EXTRA-VIRGIN) No, buying extra-virgin olive oil does not make up for your sins. But it does promise that you'll pour higher-quality oil. Oil gains "extra-virgin" status when ripe olives are "first-pressed" (lower-grade olive oils are made from the leftovers), "cold-pressed" (i.e., the oil is squeezed out of the olive naturally through pressure), and contain almost no acidity. Virgin olive oil is also first-pressed oil, but it has higher acidity levels. Flavors in olive oil vary dramatically, but it's personal preference that makes one oil better than another. Buy what you like, but remember: like balsamic, with olive oil you get what you pay for, so don't skimp. Olive oil is a key ingredient for cooking and salad dressings. When it's good quality, it's also a great bread dip; pour a generous amount into a small decorative dish and serve it solo or add a splash of balsamic, hot pepper flakes, herbes de Provence, minced garlic, tapenade, or all of the above. Lazy, but want the benefits of seasoning? Buy flavored oil. Either way, set out bite-size French bread slices and watch your guests soak it up.

OLIVES Whether dumped into a decorative bowl, tossed into pasta, or skewered for martini service, olives add fantastic flavor to any fete. Besides, they require absolutely no preparation, have a long shelf life, and don't need to be refrigerated until you've opened the jar. Buy an array— ideally from bulk in oil, which are cheaper, fresher, and need to be refrigerated, or bottled in brine. Using the bottled variety? Save the juice for "dirty" martinis (see the Classic Martini recipe in Chapter 10). If you serve them solo, don't forget to supply napkins and a small empty bowl for disposal of the pits. It's a sign of sloppy service when guests are forced to ditch them in cocktail napkins, empty glasses, or your potted plants.

PASTA Tossed with tasty accoutrements, pasta is a tummy filler as pasta salad and a lunch or dinner dream come true when the cupboards are borderline bare. You can make excellent pasta lunches by throwing canned clams, olive oil, garlic, and white wine together with linguine or wow gourmand guests with Wolfgang Puck's five-minute angel hair pasta with a cream-based sauce (see Chapter 7). If you're in a main-course pinch, dig through your party pantry basics (like olives, red peppers, olive oil, sausages, or salami) and/or any dairy and produce in the fridge (milk, cream, cheese, herbs, veggies), throw them over cooked pasta, season, and serve. See Chapter 7 for inspiration and simple sauces.

PEPERONCINIS Pickled, in the bottle, and preserved for a long shelf life, these cute red chilies are a racy addition to your antipasto plate. Or stick one on a toothpick and add a swizzle with sizzle to your martini.

PITA Yes, the Middle Eastern flatbread known for its pocket-and-hummus partnership gets stale. But if you keep it frozen and then thaw it at party time, you can cut it into tempting triangles and toast them in the oven with a dab of olive oil to make crispy chips ideal for dips.

PUFF PASTRY DOUGH It's the requisite ingredient for last-minute desserts with a homemade hook. See Puff Daddies in Chapter 9.

ROASTED RED PEPPERS Sure, you can make these by roasting fresh bell peppers under the broiler until the skins brown and blister and then spend many messy minutes trying to peel them by hand. But impatient party hostesses count on the jarred variety, which goes great with tapenade, goat cheese, and crackers or garlic toasts (for the latter see the Tiny Toasts and Crostini recipe in Chapter 5). Toss them atop pizza (see Party Girl Pizza in Chapter 5), tuck them into sandwiches, and serve them as side-kicks for cheese plates.

SALAMI Think of it as wonder meat. Unopened it can keep longer than you can maintain the party-girl lifestyle, which means it'll wait patiently in the pantry until you need it. An absolute dream when you don't have time to hit the store, it's great when sliced thin and served with cheeses, crackers or breads, and crudités (a fancy word for raw vegetables).

SALSA Fresh salsa's great, but it won't wait on the shelf until you need it. Buy a bottled or canned variety and add it to your emergency provisions. Stash it with a sealed bag of tortilla chips, and when all else fails, this classic combination will be your rescue remedy.

SAUSAGES No, not those greasy, chewy gray little wieners next to the Oscar Mayer bacon. I'm talking gourmet sausages in flavors such as smoked chicken with sun-dried tomatoes, Thai chicken with ginger, and chicken-apple. Stick them in the freezer, pull them out when it's party time, and serve them with an array of mustards and other compatible sauces.

SODAS AND SPARKLING WATER Bubbly things in single-serving bottles are great nonalcoholic alternatives. Stock up on various fruit-flavored sparkling waters, which are far more elegant than classic colas. Also great are ten-ounce bottles of Schweppes tonic and soda water, which do double duty as bar mixers and refreshing nonalcoholic beverages. When hosting a luncheon, go the refined route with 750 ml bottles of Le Village sparkling lemonade—they're all-natural, pretty in pink or pale yellow, and have way-too-cute old-fashioned pop-tops. I'm also a San Pellegrino fan. Served with lime, it's fizzy and formal and it adds an oh-so-chic European sensibility to lunch or dinner. Plus it looks good on the table.

SPREADS Spreads come in all kinds of flavors and textures: red pepper, olive (see the "Tapenade " entry in this list), hummus (for a recipe see Aimee's Hummus in Chapter 5), pesto, artichoke, and more depending on where you shop and what they stock. Check the gourmet section in your local grocery store, snatch up the best jarred spreads, and stick them in the back of your cupboard until you need a quick companion for breads, crackers, and Crudités (see Chapter 5). Need to make your limited supply last or want to liven up your spread? Add olive oil and herbs and make your own custom blend.

SUGAR AND SPICE The Party Girl Pantry is all about surviving an entertainment emergency with style. But a seasoned party thrower finds time to add homemade touches to even the most last-minute fete; thus, spices and baking basics are a must. If you follow recipes when you cook, you'll naturally acquire an impressive collection of ingredients over time. But the most basic starter set includes salt, peppercorns and a grinder, sugar (for coffee and desserts), powdered (a.k.a. confectioners') sugar (to sprinkle over desserts for visual effect), and good unsweetened baking cocoa (desserts, hot cocoa, and sprinkled visuals).

SUN-DRIED TOMATOES A best friend for goat cheese, salads, antipasto, and sexy pasta salads, sun-dried tomatoes are best bottled and packed in olive oil. They're more expensive than the dried variety but far more tender and less chewy.

TAPENADE A fancy word for olive spread, the Provençal olive-based paste jazzes up toasted slices of French bread and crackers, especially when served with goat cheese and sun-dried tomatoes. Create a refreshing contrast by pairing it with crisp vegetables such as cucumber slices, celery sticks, or radish cubes.

TEA The gourmet-coffee craze was the '90s. Today's trend is a barrage of tea blends, which is good news for us party girls, since all we need to do is boil water and it's literally in the bag. Keep a variety in the cupboard—from caffeinated basics like English Breakfast and Earl Grey and herbal blends of chamomile or mint to exotic finds like fruit-flavored and green teas. Serve them in a pretty little box or basket or on a plate and let your guests pick. Better yet, get adventurous and buy exotic whole-leaf blends and have a good old-fashioned tea party. (In this case you'll have to invest in a teapot and/or tea balls or strainers; see the Resource Guide for more details.)

TOMATO SAUCE When your cocktail party turns into a spur-of-the-moment sit-down dinner, a jar of tomato sauce and some pasta can save the day. Make a "pantry pasta" by customizing your store-bought sauce with fresh vegetables, olives, cheese, meat, or anything else that adds flavor and flare. You can also add sauce to the appetizer tray when spread on bread, covered in cheese, and toasted in the oven.

TOOTHPICKS Stick them in bite-size sandwiches and martini olives to make the goodies more manageable, and in cakes to see if they're done (if there's batter on the toothpick, leave the cake in the oven a while longer). Also offer them to guests when they have a proverbial bug in the grille (i.e., food in their teeth).

TORTILLA CHIPS They aren't exactly sexy, but few people can deny the allure of these crunchy vehicles for salsa and guacamole. Serve them with style: buy red, white, and/or blue chips, mix them together, and stack 'em high in a glass bowl or woven basket. A big bonus: unopened, they keep for a long, long time.

Party Girl Perishables

Most hosts give themselves at least enough time to make a store run before the first guests arrive. If you're fortunate enough to fall into that category and you also have a reasonably stocked pantry, grab a few of the following fresh items at the store to round out your party platter.

BREAD Bread offers huge returns on a small investment because it's filling and affordable. If you're expecting a crowd, an array of exotic loaves can guarantee that when the party's over, you'll have bread in the belly and in the bank. Buy a sweet French baguette—the long, thin kind that's milder in flavor than tangy sourdough and that when sliced can easily pop

---

PARTY GIRL PERISHABLES

· ·

| Bread | Crudités | Lemons | Milk or half-and-half |
| Cheese | Fun fruit | Limes | Pâté |

into the mouth in one bite. It can quickly become crunchy Crostini (see the Tiny Toasts and Crostini recipe in Chapter 5) or simply be sliced to buddy up with Brie or olive-oil dip. Or grab a walnut or olive loaf to accompany an array of cheeses.

Whatever you do, purchase the best quality from the best bakery available to you. Before buying, give it a squeeze. Fresh bread is like many men: a hard crust but, with a little push, obviously soft in the middle. You can turn your perishable bread into ever-ready edibles if you plastic-wrap and freeze it while it's fresh. When you want to use it, sprinkle it with a little water and thaw it in the oven at a very low heat (however low you can go). Slice, toast, and you go-go, girl.

CHEESE Serve a few great cheeses and you're a superstar. I'm not talking basic Jack and cheddar, but in an everyday grocery-store emergency you can easily get away with semisoft cheeses such as smoked Gouda or fontina or easily spreadable and tangy goat cheese. If you're lucky enough to live near a shop with a serious cheese section, ask the experts there for suggestions on exotic, flavorful, and diverse selections. They'll often offer tastes, give great advice on complementing crackers and fruits, and probably send you home with outstanding cheeses. My local store doesn't have an extensive selection, but I almost always grab a slab of rich and creamy Morbier—a fine French cheese characterized by its center layer of charcoal—and a goat cheese log. The good stuff isn't cheap, but consider the upside: all you need to do is unwrap it and put it on a platter—ideally with fruit, crackers, and bread.

Choosing cheese can be daunting, since there are hundreds of domestic and international brands on the market. To get an edge on your next wedge, be adventurous: taste at cheese shops and try something new during visits. In the meantime, following are a few readily available options that will perk up your party platter when served with bread or crackers and a knife to spread. Don't forget to always serve cheese at room temperature, and just say no to cheese cubes, a serious dairy don't for any fashionable host. Also, if it's too much to memorize the fancy foreign cheese names, serve your wedges with their labels next to them. Social butterflies should be having too much fun spreading their wings for cheese pop quizzes.

- **Blue cheese:** The most famous of the powerful blue polka-dotted cheeses made from goat, sheep, or cow's milk is Roquefort (from France and made from sheep's milk). Blue cheeses generally have a crumbly character and zingy acidic and salty flavor that might be too much for fair-weather cheesehounds. But it's the bomb when sprinkled on salad or breads with spreads, cooked into quiches, crumbled into endives (see Elegant Endives in Chapter 5), and stuffed into the mouths of cheese lovers.

- **Brie ("bree"):** Scandalously creamy, a slab or wheel of this gooey cow's-milk cheese with a soft edible rind literally oozes decadence. Flavor (often mild and nutty) and texture (ideally oh-so creamy) vary with the price tag, so ante up for the best results. FYI: Brie can also be made with goat or sheep's milk, and "triple cream" is the most indulgent style.

- **Camembert:** Creamy, ripe, and packed in a cute round box, this cow's-milk cheese with a Brie-like texture is a crowd pleaser.

- **Cheddar:** Skip the rubbery supermarket stuff and go for a good-quality slab of aged cheddar. Smooth, firm, and ranging in color from white and pale or golden yellow to orange, it can be mild or explode with sharp, somewhat salty, and acidic flavors.

◆ **Chevre ("SHEHV-ruh" or "shehv"):** French for *goat*, this usually creamy goat cheese has a citrusy-tart tang and a diner-friendly disposition. Most commonly available in an edible log shape or in tubs seasoned with herbs and spices, it's great to spread on crusty bread or sprinkle on salad or pasta.

◆ **Feta:** Greece's favorite is semifirm, inoffensive, crumbly, salty, and made from sheep, goat, or cow's milk. It's also an exception to the no-cube rule, provided you're tossing it into tomato-and-cucumber salads. Nowadays you can find good domestic versions as well as exotic interpretations from as far off as Bulgaria.

◆ **Fontina:** Semifirm and somewhat earthy, this sliceable yellow selection with small holes and a thin, oily, inedible rind can join the cheese plate or melt your heart in a grilled cheese sandwich.

◆ **Gouda:** Even picky kids don't pinch their noses at this firm cow's-milk cheese that originated in the Netherlands and has a mild to medium nutty flavor. Try aged Gouda for amazingly deep and rich flavor.

◆ **Gruyère:** It's not just for fondue, even though it is somewhat sweet and nutty and melts in your mouth, not in your hands. (Yes, it's great for melting.) "Groo-YEHR" makes for darned-good eating when sliced with fruit and nuts or tucked into quiches, or all by its sultry, firm cow's-milk self.

- **Havarti:** One of the safer supermarket bets, this Danish descendant is semisoft, holey, and mild. It's a trusty cracker companion and killer grilled cheese sandwich component.

- **Manchego:** No doubt Don Quixote had his fill of this delicious dry ewe's-milk marvel in its hometown of La Mancha, Spain. Despite its hard exterior and interior, this mild cheese is a lover, not a fighter. Make romance in your mouth: stop by a cheese specialty shop and pair it with a slab of quince paste—a hardened jamlike spread made of quince. A good party girl never misses an opportunity to wow guests with little-known wonders, and this duo is one of them.

- **Morbier ("mohr-be-YAY"):** Its trademark streak of ash or charcoal dresses up this semisoft, earthy, and seductive cow's-milk cheese. Slap down a slab next to crusty bread and watch it disappear.

- **Mozzarella:** Made from buffalo or cow's milk, elastic and mild mozzarella is more than a prized pizza topping or string-cheese sensation. If you can afford it, skip the packaged factory-made blocks and forge the fresh and delicate handmade cheese balls sold in their whey (the watery part of the milk that's separated during production). Slice it into thin slabs, serve it with tomatoes (when in season), and fall in love.

- **Parmesan:** This very hard and dry cow's-milk cheese is fully fruity and salty, and divine when grated or shaved and sprinkled over pasta and salads. But it's also fab company for a dessert course or Suzanne Goin's Parmesan-Stuffed Dates (see Chapter 5). For the best flavor avoid the less expensive and flavorless American preshredded packages and buy an imported wedge (a.k.a. Parmigiano-Reggiano).

CRUDITÉS Plainly put, "kroo-dee-TAYS" are raw or blanched (boiled very briefly) vegetables, cut for bite-size cuteness and arranged with a creative eye. They may not seem exciting on their own, but they're inexpensive, colorful, crunchy, and light, and with an astounding dip they could almost steal the show. Besides, they make for a bountiful table and are a healthy alternative to the more love-handle-friendly foods you're probably serving. At cocktail parties always pile a platter high with veggies—alternating colors for most vibrant decoration—surrounding a centerpiece dip. Think raw baby carrots, celery sticks, radishes, zucchini spears, mushrooms, bell peppers, snap peas, and individual endive leaves, as well as blanched broccoli, green beans, and asparagus. For more details see the Crudités recipe in Chapter 5.

FUN FRUIT So straightforward that it's almost silly, fruit is an idyllic accompaniment to cheeses, crackers, dessert, and other fun finger foods. I usually stay away from sticky stuff and unwieldy fruits that threaten perfectly applied lipstick and liner. But when I simply must serve sticky Pineapple with Fiery Sugar Dip (see Chapter 9), which happens with some frequency in summer, I slice 'em into bitable pieces and include a thick stack of napkins. Get seedless grapes, strawberries, blueberries, and fresh currants, which make for stellar plate decorations. Apples brown quickly when sliced and served solo (Tip: sprinkle with a little lemon juice to impede browning), but they're great in salads and perfect for Puff

Daddies (a.k.a. Fast Fruit Tarts; see Chapter 9). Whatever you do, stay in season with your fruit selection. If you've ever bitten into a pithy cardboard-flavored apple, you know the importance of ripe and ready fruit.

LEMONS Your main squeeze for cocktails, sodas, waters, and seafood, lemons are also a great dish and glass decoration. See "Whimsical Lemon Wheels" in Chapter 10 for a simple way to cut fancy circles.

LIMES If the bar's going to be open, limes should be in the shopping bag. It's a cocktail's most popular companion and a tart sidekick for Mexican dishes and beers. Since they're expensive and cocktails require little more than a nice squeeze of lime, cut them conservatively: quarter them, and then cut each quarter into thirds. That's twelve cocktail companions per lime.

MILK OR HALF-AND-HALF Coffee and sugar aren't complete without it. When offering only one, go with low-fat milk. It's the middle ground for pleasing fans of high- and non-fat dairy. Show your coffee some respect: stay away from funky flavored dairy products.

PÂTE Rich, smooth, and oh-so decadent, a slab of pâte goes a long way, whether it's made with duck or goose liver, fish, or vegetables. If you're like me, you'll rationalize a few quality-control tastes, but just be sure to save some for your guests.

✳ Bar Keeps

Who has time or money to maintain a full bar? Even in the best circumstances, supplying libations is a costly endeavor. But what's worse is buying them in an overpriced liquor store because you didn't plan in advance. When building your bar, stay away from pricey corner stores and buy your booze from discount superstores. Pick one or two pretty high-end bottles for fashion and function, and supplement them with the unfashionably huge bottles that go the drinking distance. A plentiful bar is always better than a top-shelf bar that's bound to run dry.

Another way to keep the liquid pleasures from draining your liquid assets is to stick with a one-drink theme when you entertain and supplement the centerpiece cocktail with wine and beer. Not only is it easy on the bartender (i.e., you), but also it stops you from having to sport for various spirits and mixers. Plus, a featured cocktail curtails guests' wine consumption, and—glass per glass—wine costs far more than a bottle of booze and a few mixers.

One final word of money-saving advice: You're already cutting into your fashion funds to host the throw-down, so the least your party people can do is kick in for the libations. Instead of blowing out the party budget on booze, ask guests to bring a bottle of wine or spirits, and keep backup bottles on hand. It's completely appropriate to encourage your friends to ante up to the cocktail collection—especially if they aren't polite enough to ask. For tips on how to drop a bottle-bringing hint without opening your lipstick-lined mouth, see Chapter 1.

To be best prepared for your next fiesta, cruise the following list of booze and matching mixers as well as Chapter 10, "Liquid Pleasures," and make your shopping list. And remember: Sides of nothing but salt and lime are acceptable only among friends who will love you even when you're shamefully sloppy in your bar service and speech. Keep your liquor in good company with ample supplies of one or more mixers.

BEER So what if some girls skip beer in fear of bloating. Beer is to that hunky babe what martinis are to the "Sex and the City" set. One of my handsome wine-savvy bachelor friends tells me he'd propose on the spot if he arrived at a party girl's pad and was offered a bottle of Belgium's finest with accompanying logo glasses. Plus, a hot day and a cold one are one of life's greatest pleasures. Keep a twelve-pack in your back pocket, and remember that fashion counts here. Go bottles over cans (unless you're limited in cooler space) and a selection of light and heavier, or a mixed case of brews from around the world. And consider sides of lime wedges. They add an element of south-of-the-border festivity.

GIN As gin and I had a disagreement when I was sixteen, I've only recently made friends with this unaged spirit made from distilled grains and seasoned with herbs and spices. But it's always been a cornerstone among my friends who go for Classic Martinis (see Chapter 10) and G&Ts

(gin and tonics, usually served with a squeeze of lime) or sip Snoop-style on gin and juice.

◆ **Great mates:** tonic, soda water, limes, dry vermouth, olives, anything by Frank Sinatra, and Snoop Dogg's *Doggystyle.*

RUM Made from sugarcane juice or molasses, mostly produced in the Caribbean, and dating back to the 1600s, pirates' preferred libation is still a popular choice for walking the party plank. It ranges in color from white to bronze depending on barrel aging, is a bar staple for mixing with Coke and lime, and is also a given for blender drinks made with fresh or frozen fruits.

◆ **Great mates:** Coke and lime, a blender and any variety of frozen fruit mixed with a dash of sugar and water, soda, a hearty "Yo, ho, ho," and limbo dancing or a Buena Vista Social Club CD.

TEQUILA Its reputation for turning a mild-mannered party girl into a wild woman is not far from the truth. I've done my share of shot-induced bar-top dancing and kissing guys who were 2s at 10 P.M. and 10s at 2 A.M. Thankfully, I was beyond my hard-core hangover-inducing ways before the body-shot trend and the "Girls Gone Wild" tapings. But today this per-petual party drink made from agave plants still brings out the jubilant youth in my friends and me. Only now we drink it with mixers and in por-tions that don't force us to call each other the next day to find out what we did the night before. Pick your favorite poison—gold (aged in wood barrels, which gives it its gold color) or silver (aged without wood barrels) and ideally of palatable quality—and make Maui Margaritas or Thai Mar-garitas (Chapter 10).

◆ **Great mates:** orange juice, salt, limeade, Triple Sec, limes, ibuprofen, and condoms.

TRIPLE SEC This sweet orange-flavored liqueur is good to keep around for oomph in blender drinks, margaritas, and flavored martini drinks. (Think cosmo.) It's also the poor man's Grand Marnier.

VODKA It's flexible due to the unaged grain alcohol's colorless, odorless, flavorless character, works well with fruit juices, and is critical for Bloody Mary breakfasts, vodka martinis, and cosmos. Buy the fancy frosted bottles or grab a bargain brand, but be aware that the biggest differences between cheap plastic-bottle options and prima-donna premium brands are price and image. The rest—from the taste to the hangover—is pretty much the same, especially when combined with mixers. In a recent price comparison, college-classic Popov cost $7.40 per liter at my local store, while Belvedere cost $42. I've known bartenders who pour well (cheap) vodka into name-brand bottles and swear their clients have no idea. (Not so simple for flavored vodka.) If you are comfortable filling your high-end bottle with low-end booze, go for it. Personally, I'm a terrible liar and an affected consumer; thus, I pay the price for name-brand-vodka vanity.

◆ **Great mates:** cranberry juice, orange juice, grapefruit juice, lemonade, limeade, and dry vermouth and olives, limes, and lemons, and Earth, Wind & Fire's greatest hits.

WHISKEY A great grain alcohol divided into subcategories including bourbon, Scotch, and rye, whiskey is a big-girl's drink with distinctive flavor and hard-core party-girl potency. Bourbon is Kentucky's corn-based whiskey creation. It's got a toasted, caramelized flavor and brown coloring due to aging in charred white oak barrels. I go basic and add Coke or make magnificent mixes such as Mint Juleps, Manhattans, and Bourbon Highballs (all in Chapter 10). Scotch whisky (Scots spell *whiskey* without the *e*) is Scotland's cocktail contribution, with various production styles that determine what ends up in the bottle. Its most coveted category is the "single-malt" Scotch, which means it is not blended with other whiskeys and is made at an individual distillery. These are specialty types often stocked in high-end bars and sipped solo. Blended Scotch whiskies are made for mixed drinks like the tasty and simple Johnnie Walker Black and Soda sipper recommended by a cute guy I met on Match.com (see Chapter 10).

◆ **Great mates:** ice, coffee, soda, and a faux fur rug in front of a fireplace.

WINE Yes, there are thousands to choose from, and yes, each is unique. But in the end, wine is nothing more than fermented grape juice. Who cares if you don't know the difference between merlot and malbec. That doesn't mean either one won't go down just as nicely with tonight's barbecue. I spent years dining and drinking in world-renowned restaurants before I learned that Sancerre was not only a region in France but also essentially a French word for sauvignon blanc. And I enjoyed both wines along the way.

Find a discount wine shop selling an inexpensive ($7 to $15) wine you like, buy a case of it (often accompanied by a twelve-bottle discount if you ask), store it in a cool shaded place, and be sure to restock often enough that at least six expendable bottles are on hand at all times. A proper party girl always has wine to serve and never arrives at a dinner party without a bottle for the host. But take it from this go-girl who has parted with her reserve stash or paid too much in a pinch, you'll save time, money, and your special-occasion bottles with preventive purchasing. For the best deals look to Chile, Argentina, Italy, and Spain. These countries make good-quality wines that tend to cost less than those from France, California, and Australia. Also, see Sangria (Chapter 10) for how to turn ultracheap stuff into chic party punch.

Bargain Buys and Splurge-Worthy Standouts

One last thought before you rush out to stock your Party Girl Pantry: Most towns have giant discount supermarkets that, instead of Lawrence Welk–style pop music and didactic shopping displays, offer a warehouse wonderland selling bonus-size portions of everyday groceries at bargain prices. There's no better place to buy necessary items such as napkins, toilet paper, basic candles, beer, spirits, wine, and soda. The savings will more than make up for the torture of ramming your way through the crowded aisles. Another way to save pennies is to purchase generic ingredients that don't differ in quality when bought in the cheapest form (usually in bulk or with generic labels). Buy sugar, flour, raw nuts, spices, olives, and herbs in bulk or by no-name brands. Likewise unflavored vodka as well as soda and tonic waters. On the other hand, price and producer can mean the difference between outstanding quality and a flavor flop when it comes to coffee, scented candles, chocolate, balsamic vinegar, olive oil, Scotch, and cheese. For those products, definitely splurge.

FUNDS HAVE NOTHING to do with the success of your party. To confirm that point, I need only think about the weddings I've attended. From $60,000 wine-country wonderlands to multimillion-dollar celebrity throw-downs complete with Nicholson and Beatty, live elephants, and unlimited Cristal champagne, my favorite wedding by far was a 120-person event that cost $3,000, including the bridal gown. It was at a rustic ski lodge outside of Lake Tahoe, California, where the grounds were graced with jam jars filled with wildflowers and the couple exchanged vows on a cliff overlooking Donner Lake. Afterward, guests feasted on a buffet of grilled meats and vegetables prepared by friends and then danced in the dusk to a zydeco band, drank around a bonfire, and slipped into bunk beds in the wee hours. Without the canned wedding bells and whistles, the party honored the couple rather than the caterer. In my mind you can't put a price tag on personal touches, but anyone can afford them. Insert your style and heart into your soiree and all your guests will live large.

A-List Appetizers

A GREAT PARTY doesn't have to be perfect. In fact, often absolutely imperfect parties have the best entertainment value and make the best memories. My favorite example is a formal dinner I attended at Ol Donyo Wuas, a delightfully rustic-chic ranch on 250,000 acres of Kenyan "bush." At the table were a newly-wed couple from Mexico City, a Kenyan couple who managed the resort, the proprietor's wife and her children's tutor, two men who ran a resort in Tanzania, and me, the lone California journalist. We were seated in the open-air dining room perched atop a plateau and overlooking a grove of acacia trees and hundreds of miles of pristine golden plain when the first rain of the season began. It was a light rain, one that came and went faster than my first glass of wine and without fanfare from the dinner party. Casual conversation continued while the staff stood at attention or served us with the formality of English butlers. The first time something tapped me on the back, I thought it was nothing. The second time, I looked around perplexed, since there was no one behind me. The third time, it was already apparent what was going on. Hundreds of locusts the size of Shaquille O'Neal's big toe hit us like a hailstorm. They ricocheted around the room like bullets hitting metal, wriggled their spindly legs through the salad, kerplunked into glasses, and stood like broaches on my host's lapel and the bride's back.

Aghast, I looked around for empathy and direction. I had no idea how to react to such an unsettling arrival of uninvited guests. But to everyone else at the table, the nuisance seemed about as disturbing as a few flies loose in the dining room. They continued eating and chatting about the day's safari and the next morning's "bush breakfast" as the groom casually swiped a large specimen off his wife's strapless dress, the hostess nonchalantly brushed away her living jewelry, and the baby-sitter flicked a locust off her shoulder straight into the fireplace's flames without even looking. I decided to make the best of it. I attempted in vain to fish a perpetrator out of my wine and ignored the large insect standing two inches from my plate and staring me down. When I felt a thud on the top of my head, I knew that even though nobody cracked a smile, the whole table was aware that I was now donning a locust tiara. Horrified and unable to find the nerve to reach up and grab it, I tilted my head toward the Tanzanian innkeeper and confidently asked, "Would you be so kind?" He obliged.

Toward the end of the evening I thanked my hosts with complete sincerity for the most memorable experience of my trip. Yes, during my Kenyan adventures I spotted cheetahs and white and black rhino and caught the scent of lions that saw me long before I saw them. But even now, nothing compares to my locust dinner, which became hilariously funny the second I got over the fact that I wasn't going to be able to finish my wine. The next time the proverbial fly gets into your soup, remember that if you make the best of it, your guests will, too, not to mention depart with a great story.

*

Appetizers make a big impression—especially when they're home-made. If the Palm Pilot indicates you've got a little time, put it toward one or two of the following dishes. Selected for their fab factor, and organized from effortless to most adventurous (but still easy), these starters for all occasions are flavorful, stylish, and perfect for the hostess who wants to be the mostest even when she's dashing off for a pre-party mani-pedi. Feeding a small army of famished party warriors? Just double or triple any of the recipes.

A word to the kitchen-weary: Don't be intimidated if some of the ingredients or preparations are foreign to you. Trust me, their bite is bet-ter than their bark. And with a little practice even multistep recipes will become second nature.

Elegant Endives

This is about as easy as entertaining gets, with big bonus points for its refined presentation and luscious flavors. Hand-feed one—or ten—to someone you want to seduce or friends you want to impress. FYI: Bel-gian endives (say "EN-dives" or "AHN-deeves") are slightly bitter leaves. They're crunchy, compact, and light green to white in color, and they act as an edible spoon.

TOTAL TIME: 10 minutes
ACTIVE TIME: 10 minutes
Makes about 10 to 15

Get It

1 head endive

1 cup blue cheese, crumbled

½ cup Caramelized and Spiced Nuts, chopped (see following recipe)

3 tablespoons honey

Go, Girl

◆ Slice off the base of the endive and separate the endive leaves, carefully pulling them apart so they're intact.

◆ Lay the leaves on a large serving tray in a decorative pattern—such as concentric circles or diagonal rows.

◆ Fill the base of each leaf (the strongest and whitest part) with a heaping teaspoon of blue cheese crumbles. Sprinkle each with nuts and top with a drop or two of honey.

◆ Now slip into something slinky.

✴ Caramelized and Spiced Nuts

These fancy flavored nuts require almost no effort. Prepare 'em in advance, store 'em in a well-sealed container, and when the time is right, let your salads, desserts, and cheese plates go nuts with sugar or spice or both. To only "caramelize" the nuts, skip the cayenne and black pepper, which make them "spiced."

TOTAL TIME: 5 minutes

ACTIVE TIME: 5 minutes

Makes 1 cup

Get It

2 tablespoons unsalted butter

1 tablespoon sugar

Pinch of cayenne and freshly ground black pepper (for spiced nuts)

1 cup pecans or walnuts

Go, Girl

◆ In a small saucepan melt the butter over moderate heat, add the sugar (and spices if you wish), and stir until the sugar's dissolved. Add the nuts, stirring until golden, 2 to 4 minutes.

◆ Transfer the nuts to a bowl to cool.

✳ Toasted Nuts

Nuts are tasty, but toasted they're richer, nuttier companions for salads, entrees, desserts, and anything else on which you'd like to fling a few.

TOTAL TIME: 8 to 20 minutes

ACTIVE TIME: 3 minutes

Makes 1 cup

Get It

1 cup raw walnuts, pine nuts, almonds, pecans, peanuts,* or whatever kind you like (I find walnuts the most versatile.)

If your peanuts still have skins, after they've been toasted, wrap them in a clean dish towel and roll them around inside the towel. The skins will come off—and blow all over your kitchen if you're not careful.

Go, Girl

◆ Preheat the oven to 350°F.

◆ Throw your nuts onto a baking sheet (single layer, please), and pop 'em in the middle of the oven.

◆ Bake them until they're golden brown and fragrant. For petite pine nuts it can be as fast as 8 minutes. Meatier walnut halves require about 20 minutes. Whatever you do, use a timer (seriously) and check their status often. Preoccupations have proved to this party girl that nuts go from brown to black in seconds. When they're burned, even a starving squirrel would balk at their bitterness. For Caramelized and Spiced Nuts, see the previous recipe.

✳ Suzanne Goin's Parmesan-Stuffed Dates

I met chef Suzanne Goin before she became famous for her Los Angeles restaurant Lucques. It was 1997 and I was part of a cooking club that included an art gallery owner, a banker, a wealthy model turned scholar, and me, the journalist who, for reasons too involved to explain, was working on a "Star Trek" project at Paramount Pictures. Once every two months, one of us would host a dinner and try to outdo the last. We were on our second round at the art dealer's house when he sneaked Suzanne into the mix—and his kitchen—without telling us she'd worked with some of the most important chefs of our generation (including Alice Waters of Berkeley's Chez Panisse and Mark Peel and Nancy Silverton of L.A.'s Campanile, if you care). The food was astounding that night. It was an unfair tactic for our cooking competition, but believe me, none of us complained. Without further adieu, Suzanne's simplest of pleasures.

TOTAL TIME: 5 minutes
ACTIVE TIME: 5 minutes
Serves 4

Get It

16 dates
¼-pound hunk of good-quality Parmesan
A little good-quality olive oil and arugula leaves or parsley sprigs if you
  want to be fancy

Go, Girl

◆ Cut a slit in each date and remove the pit.
◆ With a dull knife cut random hunks of Parmesan (slightly larger than the size of an almond) off your block of cheese.
◆ Slip a piece of cheese into each date; if desired, garnish with olive oil and arugula or parsley.

✳ Crudités

"Kroo-dee-TAYS" is a French term for raw veggies served as a snack and often accompanied by a dip. Aside from being affordable and effortless to prepare (especially if you buy them precut into bite-size pieces), they offer a healthy, crunchy contrast to lots of richer, more melt-in-your-mouth cocktail fare. Take advantage of these nice nibbles. Creatively arranged with rotating colors, they're beautiful and essential additions that help fill up tummies without emptying your pocketbook. Load up your tray with some or all of the following and serve them with Tarragon Dip, Wicked-Good White Bean Dip, or Aimee's Hummus (all in this chapter), or any other dip that makes you flip.

TOTAL TIME: 10 minutes
ACTIVE TIME: 10 minutes
Serves as many as you like

Get It
Baby carrots
Celery sticks, halved lengthwise and cut into 4-inch slivers
Sliced red, yellow, and/or green bell peppers
Cucumber spears
Zucchini
Mushrooms
Endive leaves
Radishes
Green beans, blanched
Asparagus spears, blanched
Broccoli, blanched
Cauliflower, blanched

Go, Girl
◆ Break out a big tray, and arrange the veggies around a centerpiece dip. *Fini!*

To "blanch" vegetables, throw them in a pot of boiling water for a minute or two, or just long enough that they've softened a little but still have their crunch. Then immediately transfer them to a cold-water bath to stop them from overcooking.

✳ Toast Points

Run-of-the-mill white bread becomes Rodeo Drive worthy with this toasting trick, which results in frilly-fun bread triangles that often team up with chichi appetizers like caviar, smoked salmon, or pâte.

TOTAL TIME: 15 to 20 minutes
ACTIVE TIME: 3 minutes
Makes 16

Get It
4 thin slices good-quality white bread

Go, Girl
◆ Preheat the oven to 350°F.
◆ Trim the crusts off of the bread, and cut each slice on the diagonal into quarters (as if you're cutting an *X*).
◆ Place the triangles in a single layer on a baking sheet. Bake for 10 minutes on one side, flip 'em, and bake the other side for about 5 minutes.
◆ Once they cool, you're cool.

✳ Tiny Toasts and Crostini

These are a party girl's greatest allies and the cornerstone to any small or large cocktail party. They're easy to make in mass amounts, light on the wallet, and crunchy carriers for tapenade, cheese, and anything else that needs a lift from the plate to your palate. Always make more than you think you'll need. Since you pay only about two bucks for a baguette, you can afford to be lavish. FYI, *crostini* is a chichi Italian term for tiny toasts brushed with olive oil. Skip the oil and put on a French accent and it's called *croûte* (pronounced "kroot"; French for *crust*) or Tiny Toast. Also see Bruschetta, which follows.

TOTAL TIME: 15 minutes
ACTIVE TIME: 5 minutes
Makes about 40

Get It
1 24-inch sweet baguette (Think thin and long and not the kind that's full
    of air pockets.)
¼ cup olive oil (for crostini)
1 clove garlic, peeled (optional)

Go, Girl
◆ Preheat the oven to 325°F.
◆ Cut the bread into ½-inch-wide slices.

- Spread 'em out—one layer only—on a baking sheet.
- If you want to add olive oil to create crostini, now's the time to do it: With a basting brush or a spoon, spread the olive oil over the bread slices. If you're not into it, go straight to the next step.
- Throw those suckers into the oven and bake for 10 minutes for lightly toasted bread with a soft center and crunchy edges, and for up to 15 minutes for all-around golden crunchiness.
- If you're into garlic, after removing the toasts from the oven, lightly rub their tops with a garlic clove. Cool completely.
- Stored in an airtight container in the fridge (cooled first), these tasty toasts can hang around until your next party.

For an easy and elegant cocktail snack, serve your crostini or tiny toasts on a platter or wood cutting board with a few knives and one of the following combos:

Brie and pesto

Goat cheese and chopped sun-dried tomatoes

Wicked-Good White Bean Dip (here in Chapter 5) and good-quality olives

Whole Roasted Garlic (here in Chapter 5), roasted red peppers, and breath mints

Warm Brandade Gratin (here in Chapter 5) and a dozen friends

Salmon Rillettes (here in Chapter 5) and sparkling wine

A selection of cheeses (blocks or slices—just say no to cubes!) and olives

The Jimtown Store's Fig and Black Olive Tapenade (here in Chapter 5) and salami

Bruschetta

He says "broo-SKEH-tah"; she says "brew-SHEH-tah." I say rustic Italian garlic toasts topped with marinated chopped tomato are easy and tasty no matter what their moniker. They also feed lots of people at limited expense and effort. Make more than you need. They're guaranteed to disappear faster than you can say *Ciao, Bella*. (For the record, the Italians say "broo-SKEH-tah.")

TOTAL TIME: 15 minutes
ACTIVE TIME: 15 minutes
Makes about 40

Get It
1 tablespoon minced shallot
¼ cup extra-virgin olive oil for toasts plus 2 tablespoons for
    tomato mixture
2 medium vine-ripened tomatoes, chopped
1 teaspoon balsamic vinegar (optional)
½ cup fresh diced mozzarella or feta (optional)
2 tablespoons fresh minced basil or chives
½ teaspoon salt or to taste
Pinch of freshly ground black pepper or to taste
1 24-inch baguette or oval-shaped loaf of French bread
1 clove garlic, peeled

WHAT TO DO WHEN YOUR TOAST IS TOAST

While bruschetta is browning is not the time to touch up the tootsies' nail polish. Take it from someone who's borne the brunt of burned edges: a few too many minutes in a very hot oven and your bread will be black. If you've burned 'em anyway but they look salvageable (only a little charred on the tops), scrape the blackened layer into the garbage can with a knife. It's a messy business, but if you're out of time, it's the only alternative to dashing back to the store or renaming your appetizer Chopped Tomato Salad.

Go, Girl

◆ Sauté the shallot in the 2 tablespoons olive oil until the shallot is tender but not browned.

◆ In a bowl mix the shallot and oil, tomatoes, balsamic, cheese, basil or chives, salt, and pepper to your preferred taste. Set the mixture aside.

◆ With a serrated knife cut the baguette or other bread into ½-inch slices. Place them on a baking sheet and pop them under the broiler for 1 to 2 minutes, or until they are golden brown with soft centers and toasted tops.

◆ Remove the toasts from the oven, rub them with the garlic clove (Go easy, sister; this stuff is potent.), and brush or spoon the remaining olive oil over the now-garlicky toasted surface.

◆ Top each toast with a tablespoon of the tomato mix, put them out on a tray, and get on with the party.

# Whole Roasted Garlic

Pity the fool who fears this pungent-breath perpetrator. It's gorgeous, puddinglike in texture, way more mellow than raw garlic, and guaranteed to ward off vampires and advances from those who don't partake. It's just as easy to make one or ten, and the dish is a perfect partner for Crostini (earlier in this chapter).

TOTAL TIME: 33 minutes
ACTIVE TIME: 3 minutes
Makes 1 whole roasted garlic

Get It
1 head of garlic, unpeeled
1 tablespoon olive oil

Go, Girl
♦ Preheat the oven to 375°F.
♦ Carefully slice off the top of the garlic bulb so the exposed cloves have a honeycomb pattern but the shape is still intact.
♦ Pour the olive oil over the exposed cloves, and then wrap the garlic head in aluminum foil, cut-side down. Bake for 30 minutes, or until garlic is soft and squishy to the touch.
♦ Place the bodacious bulb with its brown, sweet cloves faceup on a decorative plate or a cutting board. A little pinch to the skins of the cloves and the creamy, caramelized garlic will practically jump onto your crostini.
♦ Serve warm or at room temperature.

Lucques Olives and Almonds

This is one of my all-time-favorite cocktail snacks because it's completely addictive, seemingly sophisticated, easy to make, and fun to eat with your fingers. I got hooked on it while frequenting Lucques, an L.A. hot spot where celebrity chef Suzanne Goin starts off each guest with this seductive mix. Plunk down a generous bowlful in the middle of your party (plus a bowl for the pits) and baby, you're money.

TOTAL TIME: 25 minutes

ACTIVE TIME: 5 minutes

Makes 2 cups

Get It

1 cup whole raw almonds

2 tablespoons extra-virgin olive oil

¼ teaspoon salt (You may want less; Suzanne says at Lucques they like lots of salt.)

1 cup Lucques olives (Lucques are French olives. Can't find 'em? Substitute Picholine or niçoise olives.)

A few sprigs of fresh thyme

Go, Girl

◆ Toast the almonds in a preheated 400°F oven for 15 minutes, or until they smell nutty and start to turn a dark brown. The secret is for the nuts to be very toasty but not burned.

◆ When the nuts are done, remove them from the oven and toss them with 1 tablespoon of the olive oil and the salt.

◆ Toss the olives with the remaining tablespoon of olive oil and the thyme.

◆ Mix the olive and almonds and serve in a bowl.

✳Tarragon Dip

In case you didn't know, most great dips are made of obscenely rich ingredients. Close your eyes to the calories, whip it up, and serve this light green goddess with Crudités (earlier in this chapter) or crunchy steamed asparagus.

TOTAL TIME: 5 minutes
ACTIVE TIME: 5 minutes
Makes about 2 cups

Get It
1 cup sour cream
½ cup mayonnaise
½ cup fresh tarragon, stemmed
1 tablespoon lemon juice
4½ teaspoons Dijon mustard
Salt and freshly ground black pepper, to taste

Go, Girl
◆ Toss the ingredients in a blender, *whip it, whip it good*, and serve in a pretty bowl.

Wicked-Good White Bean Dip

No need to spend lots of money on fancy store-bought bread spreads or vegetable dips when you can make this savory savior in a snap. Keep the ever-ready ingredients in the cupboard, add fresh garlic, and you're golden.

TOTAL TIME: 20 minutes
ACTIVE TIME: 20 minutes
Makes 2 cups

Get It
8 cloves garlic, peeled and halved
2 tablespoons extra-virgin olive oil
2 15-ounce cans white beans, drained and rinsed
2 teaspoons red wine vinegar
½ teaspoon salt
1 tablespoon chopped parsley (optional)

Go, Girl
◆ Carefully sauté the garlic in the olive oil in a sauté pan over medium heat, without browning it, about 10 to 15 minutes.
◆ Transfer the garlic oil to a food processor, add the beans, vinegar, and salt, and puree until the mixture is smooth.
◆ Spoon the mixture into a serving bowl, sprinkle with parsley, and serve with Crostini (earlier in this chapter), toasted pita (see Chapter 4), or Crudités (also earlier in this chapter).

Aimee's Hummus

Aimee Lee Ball is a bestselling New York writer with a big heart and killer hummus recipe. Most people who want hummus these days buy it, but if you're serving a large crowd, it's far more affordable to create your own chickpea spread and serve it with Crostini (earlier in this chapter), toasted pita triangles (see Chapter 4), or Crudités (also earlier in this chapter).

TOTAL TIME: 15 minutes
ACTIVE TIME: 15 minutes
Makes 2 cups

Get It

2 cups canned chickpeas, rinsed and drained
¼ cup tahini (sesame seed paste, available at most large grocery stores)
2 teaspoons roasted garlic (see recipe in this chapter; or 2 raw cloves
    mashed to a paste with some salt)
½ teaspoon salt
¼ teaspoon freshly ground black pepper
1 teaspoon cumin powder
6 tablespoons lemon juice
Olive oil as needed to thin

Go, Girl

◆ Blend all ingredients except the olive oil well in a food processor,
adding olive oil at the end if needed to achieve your desired consistency.
◆ Serve chilled or at room temperature.

# Guacamole

Guacamole is your zesty partner for picnics, barbecues, beer and sports, and casual dinners. Other than that, there are three things you should know about making great guacamole. One: You need a good-size budget. Two: There's no such thing as enough guacamole, so plan for more than you think you'll need. And three: Buy the Hass variety of avocados. They aren't cheap, but they're way creamier than most watery and bland counterparts. I grew up—and probably out—on this guacamole. Intense and citrusy, it's not for sissies. If you want a subtler spread, start with less of the seasonings, adding a little of each at a time until it's perfect for your palate. Serve this decadent dip with thick, well-salted tortilla chips or atop Quesadillas (see the following recipe).

TOTAL TIME: 10 minutes
ACTIVE TIME: 10 minutes
Makes 4 cups

Get It
8 very ripe Hass avocados (If the flesh feels a little mushy when you push
    on the skin, you're on the right track.)
2 to 4 tablespoons lemon juice, depending on your taste preference
½ cup minced yellow onion
2 medium vine-ripened tomatoes, chopped
Tabasco
Salt

Go, Girl

◆ In a mixing bowl mash the avocado flesh with a fork or tablespoon until it's creamy—or a little chunky if you're funky.

◆ Add the remaining ingredients—a little at a time and tasting along the way if you want to monitor the intensity with the salt, Tabasco, and lemon juice.

◆ Serve your mean green in something sleek—like a color-contrasting or wooden bowl placed on a platter—and surrounded by tortilla chips.

Quesadillas

Pan-crisped tortillas filled with melted cheese, meats, veggies, and even fruit can save the day when you're low on hot items and the natives' stomachs are restless. They're a perfect kickoff to a casual dinner party. The fillings listed in this recipe are basics. Get creative and substitute Brie, papaya, and peppers; grilled steak and vegetables and Jack cheese; or whatever you find in the fridge.

TOTAL TIME: 15 minutes
ACTIVE TIME: 15 minutes
Serves 4

Get It
4 tablespoons butter or vegetable oil
8 flour tortillas

2 cups shredded Jack or cheddar cheese, or a mix of both

1 cup chopped roasted red peppers

3 cups sautéed, broiled, or grilled chicken,* shredded or chopped
   (optional)

4 sprigs of cilantro or parsley for garnish

1½ cups salsa

1 cup sour cream (optional)

*To quickly cook chicken, season pieces with salt and pepper and sauté the
chicken in strips in a pan over medium heat with a tablespoon or two of olive
oil. Or put the chicken under the broiler; cook whole breasts 10 minutes on
each side; strips should be flipped after 3 or 4 minutes.*

Go, Girl

◆ Set oven on low.

◆ Heat ½ tablespoon (1½ teaspoons) of the butter or oil in a pan over
medium heat. Flop in a tortilla, sprinkle it generously with cheese, and let
it get crisp and brown on the bottom.

◆ Add some of the red pepper and some chicken, and top with another
tortilla.

◆ Flip it, sliding another ½ tablespoon of the butter or oil under the
uncooked tortilla to help it brown.

◆ Remove the quesadilla and store it in the warm oven while you prepare the remainder—or if you're good to go, slice it like a pizza and
arrange it on a plate with a sprig of cilantro and parsley and sides of salsa
and sour cream.

◆ Ready, aim, serve.

Bite-Size Bumstead Sandwiches

Idyllic finger food for a buffet lunch or cocktail soiree, these small sandwiches put a slick spin on subs, take minutes to prepare, can feed lots of friends, and are easy to maneuver into the mouth while gabbing and holding a glass.

104

TOTAL TIME: 15 minutes

ACTIVE TIME: 15 minutes

Makes about 10

Get It

1 large sweet baguette

1 tablespoon unsalted butter, at room temperature

3 tablespoons olive paste or tapenade

⅓ cup goat cheese

⅓ pound thinly sliced turkey, smoked turkey, salami, prosciutto,
     or a combo

½ cup canned or bottled roasted red peppers, drained and patted dry

1 cup arugula or spinach, stems trimmed

10 toothpicks

Go, Girl

◆ Halve the entire baguette lengthwise.

◆ With a spoon, carefully dig out the bread's soft center from each half, leaving the crust intact.

◆ Spread the butter on the inside of the top half of the baguette. Spread the olive paste or tapenade and goat cheese along the inside of the bottom half. Stack the remaining fillings—the meat, peppers, and arugula or spinach—on top of it, until the bread hole has been filled and is almost overflowing. Cover it with the top half of the loaf.

◆ Wrap the stuffed loaf in plastic and keep it refrigerated until you're just about ready to serve.

◆ Just before you're ready to serve, preheat the oven to 300°F. Unwrap the loaf and heat it until the crust is crunchy and warm, about 10 to 15 minutes.

◆ Remove the cooked loaf from the oven and insert the toothpicks through the top to the bottom, spacing them about two inches apart lengthwise.

◆ Hold the loaf firmly and cut it into slices, with a toothpick as the centerpiece of each one. Arrange them on a platter, and get mingling.

*Oysters in the Raw

OK. So, maybe oysters are intimidating. But they're way easier to make than you think, and they're divine for special occasions and formal affairs. Plus, aphrodisiac or not, slippery mollusks served in the shell say elegant, sophisticated, and oh-so sexy. You don't need to know much about oysters to enjoy them, but at least earmark the essentials so you can purchase with pride and send your guests home feeling frisky rather than flailing with food poisoning. The dozens of types of oysters on the market range in size, shape, flavor, origin, price, and availability depending on where you live. Oysters suitable for raw revelry (not "barbecue oysters," i.e., bigger boys that are better for frying) start at 60¢ each in my neck of the burbs. Your oyster purveyor should be able to spell out the details on offerings available to you.

From the time you buy them to the moment they're shucked, oysters should be alive—with tightly closed shells or shells that shut when you tap on them—and covered with a damp cloth, allowing them breathing room in the refrigerator for no more than two days. It will take a little practice to pry them out of their shells, but you're likely to have no luck if you don't get a demo and a shucking knife first. Ask your purveyor to show you the ropes. Brave it at home, and by the third or fourth shell you'll be one bad mother shucker. Shell shocked? You can call the seafood store in advance and ask the purveyor to do the dirty work.

> **TOTAL TIME:** 20 minutes
> **ACTIVE TIME:** 20 minutes
> *Makes 12*

> Get It
> ⅓ cup white wine, champagne vinegar, or red wine vinegar
> 1 tablespoon minced shallot
> Freshly ground black pepper
> Kosher salt for display (optional; you can also use Crushed Ice Mold—
>   details follow)
> 12 fresh raw oysters

Go, Girl

◆ Prepare a mignonette ("meen-yawn-NET") sauce to accompany the oysters: Combine the wine or vinegar, shallot, and pepper, and set the sauce aside in a decorative bowl.

◆ Sprinkle a large mound of kosher salt—for decoration, not flavor—on a colored plate (contrast is key) and set it aside.

◆ Shuck the suckers (or not, if they're already done), discard the flat shell, and return the meat to the more cup-shaped shell halves.

◆ Balance the oysters on the half shell atop the salted plate and add to each a teaspoon of mignonette.

◆ Serve with cocktail napkins (it's slippery-sloppy fun), slurp them back right out of the shell, and before you know it, the party world is your oyster.

COOL CRUSHED ICE MOLD

· ·

For a way-cool way to serve oysters on ice, fill a cake pan or baking dish (any wide-based container will do) with a smooth 2- to 3-inch layer of crushed ice (add seaweed or other decorative items to the crushed ice if you like). Pack down the ice and put it in the freezer for at least a half hour. When you're ready to serve, pop the ice out of the container and use it as a plate for oysters on the half shell, shrimp, or anything else that should be kept cold. Make sure you present it on something that can contain water after the ice melts.

Flying Fish Grill Pan-Fried Oysters

While researching the restaurants of Carmel, California, for *Bon Appétit*, I found myself freaking over the fried oysters served at a discreet and friendly restaurant called Flying Fish Grill. I asked chef-owner Kenny Fukumoto for his secret, and he kindly told me to do the following.

TOTAL TIME: 20 minutes

ACTIVE TIME: 20 minutes

Makes 12

Get It

½ cup plus 2 tablespoons canola oil

1 tablespoon finely chopped onion

1 tablespoon finely chopped celery

1 tablespoon finely chopped red bell pepper

1 tablespoon oyster sauce (available at Asian markets)

½ cup water

1 cup panko (Japanese bread crumbs, available at Asian supermarkets and gourmet grocers), ground fine in a food processor or coffee grinder

1 egg, whipped

1 dozen Malpeque oysters, shucked (save the shells)

1 tablespoon toasted sesame seeds*

To toast sesame seeds, brown them for a minute or two in a sauté pan over medium-low heat.

Go, Girl

◆ In a skillet heat the 2 tablespoons oil on high heat until the oil just begins to smoke.

◆ Add the onion, celery, and bell pepper and stir quickly. Add the oyster sauce and water, and reduce slightly (i.e., simmer away some of the liquid, thus reducing it). Remove the sauce from the heat, and set it aside.

◆ Place the panko on a plate, and pour the whipped egg into a small bowl.

◆ Dip each oyster one at a time into the egg and then press the oyster into the panko, coating both sides.

◆ Heat the remaining ½ cup oil over medium-high heat, and then add the oysters and fry them until each side is just golden and crunchy but not overcooked, about 2 minutes.

◆ Place each oyster in a half shell, spoon the vegetable sauce over the top, sprinkle with sesame seeds, and serve.

✳ Party Girl Pizza

Making homemade pizza is easier than you think. But if the idea freaks you out, you can always call up your local pizza parlor and persuade the establishment to sell you some dough to go. In either case the point is to do things in your own dazzlingly different way, so think creatively when pondering your pizza toppings. This favorite is made with combinations I fell in love with at Bistro Don Giovanni in Napa Valley. But I've also rifled through the refrigerator and topped my dough with whatever I could find, which on one occasion amounted to tomato chunks, ground pork, mushrooms, olives, fresh basil, salt, and pepper. Whatever you do, take a risk with your doughy disk. And try your hand at Godfathers (later in this chapter) to make your guests an offer they can't refuse.

TOTAL TIME: 2 hours, 10 minutes
ACTIVE TIME: 20 minutes
Makes 4 8-inch thin-crust pizzas

Get It

1 package dry yeast

1½ teaspoons salt

1 tablespoon sugar

2 tablespoons extra-virgin olive oil for dough plus 4 teaspoons
   for toppings

¾ cup water

2¾ cups all-purpose flour

12 fresh figs, halved

4 slices prosciutto, quartered

¼ cup balsamic vinegar

1 cup caramelized onion (prep details follow)

3 cups arugula

Go, Girl

◆ Make the dough: Activate the yeast by carefully following the instructions on the package. In a food processor with the rubber blade or by hand, mix the salt, sugar, the 2 tablespoons olive oil, activated yeast, and water. Add the flour and mix well.

◆ With floured hands knead the sticky mass for a few minutes to ensure it's velvety smooth. Form the dough into a ball, place it in a bowl greased with olive oil, cover it with plastic wrap, and let it rise for an hour.

◆ Separate the raised dough into four equal balls, and on a floured surface roll out the balls into four thin 8-inch-round pies. (I use a rolling pin or my hands à la old-school Italians, but before I was well equipped, I used a beer bottle.)

◆ Put the pizza pies on floured baking sheets, cover them with a dish towel, and let them rest for about half an hour.

◆ Preheat the oven to 475°F. Top each pizza with 1 teaspoon of the remaining olive oil, 6 fig halves, 4 pieces of prosciutto, a hearty drizzle of

---

CARAMELIZING ONIONS

Even people who cringe at the thought of onions will cuddle up next to them when they're caramelized. Just slice a yellow onion or two and throw the slices into a skillet with a tablespoon or two of butter. Stir, cover the pan, cook for 8 to 10 minutes, or until they're a dark gold, and season with salt and pepper. Toss your now browned brothers into scrambled eggs, atop pizza, into Bite-Size Bumstead Sandwiches (see recipe earlier in this chapter), or directly into your mouth.

balsamic, caramelized onion, and a handful of arugula. Cook for 15 minutes in the upper part of the oven.

◆ Cut the pizzas into slices and serve.

Variations for Toppings
Tomato sauce, mozzarella and Gorgonzola cheese
A variety of mushrooms, tomatoes, basil, and caramelized onions
    (see accompanying box)
Pesto, pine nuts, and crumbled feta
Anything you want

✳ Wolfgang Puck's Smoked Salmon and Caviar on Buckwheat Cakes

When you really want to impress someone, break out this recipe. I first fell in love with it while cooking out of *The Wolfgang Puck Cookbook* (Random House, 1986) in my early twenties. Today the appetizer is as stylish as ever, with all the panache of classic caviar service but at a far more affordable price. Next time you want to go all-out elegant, turn to this adaptation of Wolfgang's classic. He recommends you serve these with flutes of chilled champagne. I'm with him.

TOTAL TIME: 25 minutes
ACTIVE TIME: 25 minutes
Makes 12 to 16 2- to 3-inch cakes

Get It

3 tablespoons buckwheat flour

4 tablespoons all-purpose flour

½ teaspoon salt

½ teaspoon freshly ground black pepper plus additional for topping

1 tablespoon plus a few pinches of minced fresh dill plus sprigs for
garnish

½ cup good-tasting beer at room temperature

2 tablespoons unsalted butter, melted, plus a small piece for coating
the skillet

1 egg, separated

Thinly sliced red onion

3 to 4 ounces Scotch or Norwegian smoked salmon, cut into paper-thin
slices

½ cup sour cream

2 ounces domestic golden caviar

Go, Girl

◆ Prepare the buckwheat cakes: In a mixing bowl combine the flours,
salt, the ½ teaspoon pepper, and the 1 tablespoon minced dill. Slowly stir
in the beer, melted butter, and egg yolk. In a small bowl whip the egg
white until stiff. Carefully fold it into the buckwheat batter.

◆ Heat a heavy skillet, griddle, or blini pan until a small piece of butter
dropped on the surface foams. Ladle the batter into the pan to form separate 2- to 3-inch cakes.

◆ Cook the cakes over medium heat until they're brown on the bottom,
about 2 to 3 minutes, and then turn them and brown the other side.

- Transfer the cakes to a tray or baking sheet large enough to hold them in one layer, and keep them warm.
- Assemble: On each of the cakes place a thin layer of onion. Cover the onion with a slice of salmon. Spoon a little sour cream over the salmon and top with a teaspoon of caviar. Sprinkle with the remaining minced dill and grind a little pepper over each.

114

- Presentation: Place three or four finished buckwheat cakes on warm appetizer plates. Garnish each plate with a sprig of fresh dill and serve.

The Jimtown Store's Fig and Black Olive Tapenade

California's Sonoma County may be internationally known for its wines and awesome cycling routes, but anyone who's been to the area and done it right knows that the Jimtown Store is an absolute must-stop. Party friends recently popped by my house after a visit to the gourmet general grocer and gift shop and left me with a container of this tapenade. I was so enamored that I called owner Carrie Brown and she kindly agreed to share the recipe, which I adapted from her book *The Jimtown Store Cookbook—Recipes from Sonoma County's Favorite Country Market* (Harper-Collins, 2002). Serve this sweet and salty spread with Crostini (earlier in this chapter) and friends who won't be appalled if you eat more than your share. Carrie points out that you can also pair it with lamb, pork, cured meats like prosciutto and salami, and robust goat's-milk or sheep's-milk cheeses. Make a lot and store it in the freezer for up to three months.

TOTAL TIME: 24 hours and 45 minutes

ACTIVE TIME: 45 minutes

Makes about 4 cups

Get It

2 cups (about 12 ounces) quartered dried black figs, such as Black Mission

4 cups (1 pound) pitted brine-cured black Greek olives (kalamatas),
    coarsely chopped

7 tablespoons fresh lemon juice

3 tablespoons whole-grain mustard

4 cloves garlic, peeled and chopped

2 tablespoons drained small (nonpareil) capers

4 teaspoons finely chopped fresh rosemary

2 cups extra-virgin olive oil

Freshly ground black pepper

Kosher salt

1 cup toasted pine nuts (optional; for toasting details see the Toasted
    Nuts recipe earlier in this chapter)

Go, Girl

◆ Pour 3 cups of water into a heavy medium saucepan, add the figs, and
bring the contents to a simmer over medium heat. Partially cover the pan
and cook, stirring once or twice, until the figs are very tender, about 30
minutes. Cool slightly, and then drain, reserving 1 tablespoon of the liquid.

◆ In a food processor combine the cooked figs, olives, lemon juice, mustard, garlic, capers, rosemary, and the reserved tablespoon of liquid. Pulse
to create a thick paste. With the motor running, gradually add the olive

oil. Transfer the mixture to a storage container. Season generously with pepper and add salt to taste (given the several salty ingredients, none may be required). Cover and refrigerate at least 24 hours, to develop the flavors. Before serving, bring the tapenade to room temperature.

◆ If you are using the pine nuts, stir them into the tapenade just before serving.

 ## Sautéed Diver Scallops with Cauliflower, Capers, and Almonds

Even if chef Richard Reddington weren't a total hottie, I'd have a crush on him because his food is so darned sexy. It's no wonder "The Bachelor" producers approached him to star as the first eligible babe in the reality-TV-show dating game. (He declined.) When I was dining at The Restaurant at Auberge du Soleil, Napa Valley's most romantic luxury resort, he served this refined and decadent dish. Good thing he didn't do the show: if he'd prepared these scallops for his dates, he'd have broken hearts all across America. Try it at home to woo the one you love.

TOTAL TIME: 30 minutes
ACTIVE TIME: 30 minutes
Serves 4

Get It
½ cup balsamic vinegar
Salt

2 cups cauliflower florets

¼ cup cream

4 fresh scallops, 2 to 3 ounces each (day boat, if possible)

Freshly ground black pepper

1 tablespoon extra-virgin olive oil plus enough for garnish

1½ tablespoons unsalted butter

2 tablespoons capers

2 tablespoons toasted slivered almonds

2 tablespoons golden raisins

1 tablespoon chopped parsley

Go, Girl

◆ In a small pot bring the balsamic to a boil; reduce by half, and set aside.

◆ Bring 2 quarts of water to a boil and season with salt to taste. Add the cauliflower florets and cook until tender (about 60 seconds); then shock (i.e., chill) them in an ice bath.

◆ Place 1 cup of the chilled cauliflower in a pot, add the cream, and cook for 8 minutes. Puree the creamy cauliflower in a blender or food processor. Keep it warm while you prepare the scallops.

◆ Season the scallops with salt and pepper. Warm a small sauté pan and pour in the olive oil when it just starts to smoke. Add the scallops and cook until they're medium rare, about 1 minute on each side (longer for thicker scallops).

◆ In another small sauté pan heat the butter until it begins to brown. Add the cup of nonpureed cauliflower, cook for 1 minute, season with salt and pepper, and then add the capers, almonds, raisins, and parsley.

- Place a small circle of cauliflower puree in the middle of a warmed serving plate, top with the caper-raisin ragout, and crown with the scallops.
- Garnish the plate with a drizzle of balsamic reduction and olive oil.

Godfathers

You seriously have to try this at home—especially because you won't find it elsewhere and anyone to whom you serve it will fall in love with you immediately. Less notorious than the head of the Corleone family but more addictive than old-school gangsters' hootch, Godfathers were introduced to me in 1989 at a rustic pizza parlor outside Yosemite National Park, where my friends and I downed them with pitchers of beer. Give your guests a choice between the gun, the cannoli, and these big balls of dangerously good and crusty baked pizza dough with garlic or cinnamon-sugar dipping sauce and Godfathers are the first on the take. Crack a cold one, rent Francis Ford Coppola's *Godfather* trilogy, and serve these and you're a made woman.

TOTAL TIME: 2 hours
ACTIVE TIME: 10 minutes
Serves 6 to 8

Get It
1 package dry yeast
1½ teaspoons salt

1 tablespoon sugar

2 tablespoons extra-virgin olive oil

¾ cup water

2¾ cups all-purpose flour

1 cup (2 sticks) unsweetened butter

2 cloves garlic, peeled

½ cup sugar

3 to 4 teaspoons cinnamon

Go, Girl

◆ Make the dough: Activate the yeast by carefully following the instructions on the package. In a food processor or by hand, mix the salt, sugar, olive oil, activated yeast, and water, and then add the flour and mix well.

◆ With floured hands knead the sticky mass for a few minutes to ensure it's velvety smooth. Place the dough in a bowl greased with olive oil, cover it with plastic wrap, and let it rise for an hour. Divide the dough into four equal balls, place them on a floured baking sheet, and let them rise for a half hour.

◆ Preheat the oven to 475°F. Cook the dough in the middle of the oven for 15 to 20 minutes, until the loaves are shaped like giant softballs and the crust is hardened and golden brown. (Make sure there are no racks above them, since they will continue to rise and expand as they cook.)

◆ While the Godfathers are in the oven, melt the butter in a pan over low heat and keep it warm.

◆ Get three small bowls or cups. Press the garlic (or mince it if you don't have a press) into one of them. In another bowl, combine the sugar and cinnamon.

◆ When the Godfathers are ready to come out of the oven, pour half the butter into the remaining empty bowl and the other half into the bowl with the garlic.

◆ Serve your Godfathers with the trio of bowls and show your buddies how it's done: Rip off a piece of the pizza ball, dip it into the garlic butter, and pop it into your mouth. Repeat, but this time double dip—first into the basic butter and then into the cinnamon sugar.

Salmon Rillettes

Laurent Manrique, an excellent chef with boyish good looks and manly French cooking skills, kicked off an excellent evening at San Francisco's very refined Campton Place with a dollop of this creamy-dreamy salmon spread served with minitoasts. Follow his lead to add a little yummy-sexy luxury to your luncheon or cocktail party. Add a side of Tiny Toasts and Crostini (see the recipe earlier in this chapter), or scoop the salmon spread into individual Belgian endive leaves. FYI, *rillettes* ("ree-yets") is a fancy French word for a slow-cooked appetizer spread.

TOTAL TIME: 1 hour, 15 minutes
ACTIVE TIME: 15 minutes
Makes about 1½ cups, serves about 8

Get It
1 celery stalk, sliced thin
1 onion, sliced thin
1 leek, sliced thin

1 teaspoon whole peppercorns

1 bay leaf

1 cup white wine

1 lemon, halved

6 ounces king salmon fillet

2 ounces crème fraîche (budget partyers can substitute sour cream or a
   cream-and-sour-cream combo)

2 tablespoons minced chives

3 tablespoons lemon extra-virgin olive oil

Salt and freshly ground black pepper

Go, Girl

◆ Bring a large pot of water to a simmer. Add the celery, onion, leek,
peppercorns, bay leaf, wine, and lemon and simmer for 25 minutes.

◆ Then add the salmon. Cover the pot, remove it from the heat, and let
it stand for 10 minutes.

◆ Remove the salmon and chill it in the refrigerator. Discard the vegetable water.

◆ In a food processor or by hand, whip the salmon with the crème
fraîche, chives, and olive oil, and add salt and pepper to taste. Keep the
spread chilled until you're ready to serve.

✳ Fritters with Double Yellow Dipping Sauce

These fried friends make for spectacularly savory cocktail snacks for small
to medium-size parties. I discovered a fritter recipe while working with
Domaine Chandon winery and restaurant on its website, which included

a decadent version made with crab and sparkling wine. My adaptation uses zucchini (more affordable), water (again, cash-conscious), and Double Yellow Dipping Sauce, a last-minute concoction made from ingredients I had lying around. But if you need an excuse to splurge on crab and pop a bottle of bubbly or white wine, now you have one. (Substitute ¾ pound crab for the zucchini and wine for the water.) One more thing: These are best when served and devoured immediately, but they still taste good at room temperature—especially after you've hit the champagne and you have the munchies.

TOTAL TIME: 1 hour
ACTIVE TIME: 30 minutes
Makes about 20

Get It

1¼ cups sifted all-purpose flour

¼ teaspoon sugar

¼ teaspoon salt for fritters plus a few shakes for the dip

¾ cup water (or sparkling or white wine)

2 eggs, separated

2 cups minced mango

1 cup minced yellow bell pepper

¼ cup lime juice

1 tablespoon white wine vinegar

¼ cup sesame oil

1 tablespoon minced chives

2 cups grated zucchini (or ¾ pound crabmeat)

¾ cup peanut oil

Go, Girl

◆ In a small bowl mix the flour, sugar, and ¼ teaspoon salt. Whisk in the water or wine and the yolk of one egg (discard the other yolk). Cover the bowl with plastic wrap, and set it aside somewhere warm for half an hour.

◆ While the batter is resting, you're not. Instead you're mixing the Double Yellow Dipping Sauce by combining the mango, bell pepper, lime juice, remaining salt to taste, vinegar, sesame oil, and chives. Pour the sauce into a pretty serving bowl, and set it aside.

◆ Fold the zucchini or crab into the batter.

◆ Using an electric mixer or good old-fashioned elbow grease and a whisk, whip the egg whites until they hold firm peaks; gently fold them into the batter.

◆ Set the oven on low.

◆ In a frying pan heat the peanut oil over medium-high flame, and then fry a few tablespoon-size dollops of the batter at a time, turning them over when the bottoms have browned.

◆ Put the fritters on a plate covered with a paper towel to help drain excess oil, and keep them in the warmed oven while you fry the rest.

◆ Serve as soon as possible with the Double Yellow Dipping Sauce.

Warm Brandade Gratin

This savory brandade (say "brahn-DAHD") requires planning, but it fills crowds, takes minutes to prepare, and has a huge fancy factor. Straight from San Francisco's Foreign Cinema restaurant to your party platter, the sexy spread by executive chefs Gayle Pirie and John Clark is creamy, lightly garlicky, and extremely impressive even to people who aren't fish fans. Serve it as an appetizer with Crostini (see Tiny Toasts and Crostini earlier in this chapter) or in individual ramekins if you want to be especially elegant. It doesn't take long to prepare, but it does require you to soak the fish for twenty-four hours, so get on it early or go elsewhere.

TOTAL TIME: 24 hours and 25 minutes
ACTIVE TIME: 25 minutes
Serves 8 as an appetizer spread

Get It

1 pound salt cod (cod that's been salted and dried)
5 cups milk
2 cups Yukon gold potatoes (or other potatoes), peeled and cut into
    1-inch chunks
2 bay leaves
7 cloves garlic, peeled and either pressed with a garlic press or minced
½ cup extra-virgin olive oil
¼ cup cream
Generous pinch of kosher salt

Go, Girl

◆ Soak the cod in water in the refrigerator for 24 hours, changing the water three or four times to eliminate excessive saltiness.

◆ Combine the milk, potatoes, and bay leaves in a medium saucepan and cook over medium heat for 10 minutes.

◆ Cut the cod into equal pieces, add them to the pan, and continue to cook for 8 to 12 minutes, or until the potatoes are just cooked through and the cod is tender. Remove the potatoes and cod with a strainer, cool them on a baking sheet, and discard the milk.

◆ In a food processor whip the cooked fish and potatoes. Add the garlic, olive oil, cream, and salt, and whip until smooth, fluffy, and light, about 4 to 5 minutes. Take a taste. If it needs more salt, add it now.

◆ Transfer the brandade to a broiler-safe pan, a baking dish, or single-serving ramekins and broil for 3 to 6 minutes, or until lightly golden on top.

◆ Serve with pride.

✳

I LOVE SERVING finger foods because they're easy for guests to snatch up when they do a drive-by of the snack table and especially practical when the party pad is standing room only. They also allow me to shirk plate and silverware responsibilities so long as there are plenty of napkins around. My only warning: When it comes to making finger-favorable hors d'oeuvres, always consider function over form. Even haute restaurants make the mistake of building annoyingly fragile and unwieldy tray-passed tidbits that invariably dive from their edible perches onto the floor, new blouse, napkin, or chin. Such calamities are the sign of a self-absorbed chef who prefers pomp over commonsense circumstance. Besides, even if your guests are the clods, you're the one who'll be combing bruschetta bits out of the carpet.

6

Soup and Salad Days

I ALMOST ALWAYS take salads to potluck parties because they're fresh, glamorous, and affordable to make in bulk. But when I'm at home and hankering for something warm, cheap, and likely to leave leftovers, I often turn to soup. Sure, I may open a can when I'm on deadline and starving for sustenance, but if the gals are coming over and I need to come up with something quick, I dig through my cabinets and shelves and may pull out vegetable stock or bouillon; canned beans such as garbanzo, kidney, black, and white; and fresh vegetables such as squash, tomatoes, zucchini, and corn. I boil a big pot of stock or water with bouillon, drain and rinse the beans, chop the vegetables, toss everything into the water, season it with hot pepper flakes, and serve it with sunken chunks of cheddar cheese and a dollop of sour cream. Add a loaf of crusty bread and a few friends, and I've got simple soup for the soul sisters.

*

S oups and salads are the secret weapons of the hurried hostess. They're easily glamorized and oh-so affordable, and they require very little cooking, which means you can throw them together faster than you can explain to your guests how you made such gorgeous creations. Serve the following soups or salads—organized from easiest to most time-consuming—in larger portions as lunch entrees or phenomenal first courses at dinner. But whatever you do, make sure you buy extremely fresh, good-quality greens and refrain from adding dressing to your salads until your guests are good to go. The only things that can wilt the wonder of these fresh party classics are soggy veggies that have been sitting around too long.

☀ Butternut Squash Soup

Don't be afraid of butternut squash. It may look big, hard, and cumbersome, but if you've got a sharp knife, you're the master! Besides, it's easier to prepare than you think—as long as you've got a blender—and extremely colorful and glamorous. Next time you want to kick off a formal dinner with creamy-smooth soup, remember that butternut squash is your buddy. By the way, skip the bacon if you're serving vegetarians.

TOTAL TIME: 1 hour, 15 minutes
ACTIVE TIME: 30 minutes
Serves 4 to 6

Get It

2 tablespoons unsalted butter

2 cups finely chopped onion

2 large cloves garlic, peeled and minced

1 2-pound butternut squash

2 slices bacon (optional for garnish)

2 Granny Smith apples, peeled, cored, and chopped

3 cups low-sodium chicken broth

¾ cup water

Salt and freshly ground black pepper

4 tablespoons sour cream or crème fraîche (optional)

Go, Girl

◆ In a large pot cook the butter, onion, and garlic over moderate heat, stirring occasionally, until the onion is translucent and soft, about 10 minutes.

◆ Meanwhile, peel the butternut squash with a vegetable peeler, slice it lengthwise in half, scoop out the seeds in the middle, and chop the squash into 1-inch pieces.

◆ Also, if you're opting for a bacon garnish (I recommend you do), cook the bacon now—either in the microwave, in a pan over medium-high heat, or under the broiler until it's crispy but not burned. Then cut it into small chunks.

◆ To the pot of softened onion add the squash, apples, broth, and water. Partially cover the pot, and let it simmer for 25 minutes.

- Transfer the chunky soup in batches to a blender, making sure you include enough liquid from the pot with each batch to help the squash to puree.
- Puree the soup, and then pour it into a clean saucepan and heat it. As the soup heats, season it with salt and pepper to taste. If it's too thick, add extra water.
- When you're ready to serve, transfer the soup to bowls and garnish each with a dollop of sour cream or crème fraîche and bacon.

Jean-Paul Picot's Gratinéed Onion Soup

New York chef Jean-Paul Picot is the French toque behind the Midtown Manhattan bistro La Bonne Soupe and *La Bonne Soupe Cookbook* (Hungry Minds, Inc., 1997), where I found this recipe for classic French onion soup. It's been nominated best onion soup in NYC by the *Daily News*, and it remains his most popular broth-based beauty. Serve it anytime you want to warm your tummy and your diners' hearts. And don't forget to cut your onions very thin and let them cook until they're very, very soft.

TOTAL TIME: 1 hour, 20 minutes
ACTIVE TIME: 20 minutes
Serves 4 to 6

Get It

3 tablespoons unsalted butter
4 large sweet onions (Bermuda or Spanish; about 1½ pounds total), sliced thin

1 teaspoon sugar

1 cup dry white wine

2 quarts low-sodium canned beef broth

2 ribs celery with leaves, each rib cut in half

Salt and freshly ground black pepper

¼ cup fino (very dry sherry)

4 to 6 slices baguette, cut ¼ inch thick and lightly toasted (for toasting
    directions see the Tiny Toasts and Crostini recipe in Chapter 5)

¼ cup coarsely grated Emmental, Gruyère, or other Swiss-type cheese

Go, Girl

◆ Melt the butter in a 3- or 4-quart saucepan over low heat. Add the onion slices and sugar. Cook over low heat, stirring occasionally, until the onions are lightly caramelized, 20 to 30 minutes. (The longer the onions cook slowly, the richer the flavor of the soup.)

◆ Add the wine and cook over medium-high heat until the wine reduces to about half, about 5 minutes. Add the broth, celery, and salt and pepper, and bring the liquid to a boil over high heat. Reduce the heat to low, partially cover the pan, and allow the soup to simmer until the onions are meltingly tender, about 40 minutes.

◆ Remove and discard the celery. Add the fino and simmer the soup for another 5 minutes.

◆ To serve, preheat the oven to 375°F. Ladle the soup into individual ovenproof bowls. Top each with a slice of baguette, sprinkle with a few spoons of cheese, and place the bowls on a cookie sheet. Heat the soup in the center of the oven just until the cheese melts and bubbles, 5 to 6 minutes.

◆ Carefully remove the tray from the oven and serve.

Haute House Salad

So long as you have great fresh lettuce, you don't need to dwell over fancy dressing for your salad. Follow the Italians—they know how to eat. A dash of good-quality olive oil, a sprinkle of balsamic vinegar, and a shake or two of salt and you are reliving the salad days. You can also Glamorize Your Greens as noted in the accompanying box.

TOTAL TIME: 5 minutes
ACTIVE TIME: 5 minutes
Serves 4

Get It
2 tablespoons extra-virgin olive oil
1 teaspoon balsamic vinegar or to taste
Salt
6 to 8 cups mixed lettuces, arugula, or any small green and leafy lettuce

Go, Girl
- In a serving bowl combine the olive oil, balsamic, and salt.
- Throw the salad in, toss well, and serve.

Caprese Salad

A classic Italian combination that's as bright in color as it is in flavor, this brilliant dish requires little more than three minutes and a good knife. Go for heirloom tomatoes and serve it seasonally—think summertime—

GLAMORIZE YOUR GREENS

Even if you're serving simple greens, you can say sophistication with any of these easy and glamorous additions:

Baked goat cheese: Make silver-dollar-size patties of goat cheese, dip them in olive oil, dredge them in bread crumbs, and bake them at 375°F for 5 minutes.

Seared scallops: In a small sauté pan over medium heat warm 1 tablespoon olive oil, season the scallops with salt and pepper, and cook them until they're medium rare, about 1 minute on each side.

Toasted Nuts: See Chapter 5.

Berries: Blueberries, strawberries, dried cranberries (think winter), and even grapes can add fun to balsamic-based dressings.

Sliced pears, toasted walnuts (see Toasted Nuts in Chapter 5), **and blue cheese** (serve with a vinaigrette).

Tomatoes: The fancier, the better. Stay away from the cardboard-flavored mass-produced tomatoes and go for the good stuff—heirloom or vine-ripened.

Avocados: Fan slices on the side of your salad, or toss chunks in with the greens.

Sun-dried tomatoes: Chop, sprinkle, and serve with a vinaigrette.

Cheese: Think crumbled Roquefort or fresh shaved Parmigiano-Reggiano.

when the fruit's at its best. I serve this at larger parties because it's easy to refill when necessary, provided you've got extra provisions.

TOTAL TIME: 5 minutes
ACTIVE TIME: 5 minutes
Serves 4 to 6

Get It

2 pounds (about 6 medium) vine-ripened tomatoes (ideally heirloom, in various colors such as yellow, purple, red, and orange)
1 pound fresh mozzarella cheese (shaped in balls a little smaller than baseballs, available in the deli section of good grocery stores)
2 tablespoons extra-virgin olive oil
2 tablespoons basil chiffonade (i.e., cut into thin strips; *chiffonade* is a French culinary term for shredded)
Generous pinch of sea salt

Go, Girl

◆ Cut the tomatoes and cheese into ¼-inch slices and arrange them like downed dominoes on a serving plate.
◆ Finish with a generous drizzle of olive oil and a sprinkle of basil and sea salt. *Finito!*

Mom's House Salad

I grew up on this salad and swear by it. Its vinaigrette is French in style and complex in flavor, and it has a wonderful tang thanks to the Worcestershire sauce. Keep the supplies on hand, and even at the last minute you'll soon be known for your salads.

TOTAL TIME: 7 minutes
ACTIVE TIME: 7 minutes
Serves 4

Get It

3 tablespoons extra-virgin olive oil

1 tablespoon balsamic vinegar

½ teaspoon Dijon mustard

¼ teaspoon pressed fresh garlic

2 dashes of Worcestershire sauce

Generous pinch of salt

6 cups lettuce (torn butter lettuce or arugula, mixed greens, or baby spinach)

¼ cup toasted walnuts (optional; see the Toasted Nuts recipe in Chapter 5)

½ avocado, skinned and sliced or cubed (optional)

1 medium tomato, sliced (optional)

Go, Girl

◆ Combine the olive oil, balsamic, mustard, garlic, Worcestershire sauce, and salt, and whisk until emulsified.

◆ Pour the dressing into a serving bowl, add the rest of the ingredients, toss until the dressing coats the lettuce, and serve.

# Tip of the Iceberg Salad with Blue Cheese Dressing

This oh-so-simple and classic salad balances the rich dressing with fresh and crunchy iceberg lettuce. Its luxury look makes it an elegant dinner partner. If you're lazy or super late in throwing your party together, you can always use store-bought blue cheese dressing.

TOTAL TIME: 5 to 10 minutes

ACTIVE TIME: 5 to 10 minutes

Serves 4

Get It

⅓ cup mayonnaise

⅓ cup sour cream

1½ ounces blue cheese, at room temperature

1 tablespoon fresh lemon juice

Freshly ground black pepper (lots)

½ head iceberg lettuce

1 tablespoon finely chopped fresh chives

2 slices cooked bacon, chopped, or ¼ cup toasted walnuts (optional; for toasting instructions see Toasted Nuts in Chapter 5)

Go, Girl

◆ In a bowl whisk the mayo, sour cream, blue cheese, lemon juice, and pepper until well combined. Cover and refrigerate.

- Slice the lettuce into four equal wedges, without letting each wedge fall apart.
- When you're ready to serve, place one wedge vertically on a salad plate with the outside larger leaves down and the center of the lettuce pointing up. Add a hefty dollop of dressing, sprinkle with chives and bacon or nuts, and repeat with three more plates.

✳ Caesar Salad

If you have as hard a time as I do finding a truly good Caesar salad, you'll be thrilled with this oh-so-easy recipe. Straight from Gotham Bar and Grill's very talented executive chef Alfred Portale, this tangy and bold sensation was deemed one of the Big Apple's best by *Time Out New York* and is sure to garner acclaim at your dinner table. Alfred gave me a heads up with this recipe: "The flavor of this dressing is bold, with lots of garlic and anchovy, but you can adjust the amounts to your taste." For this party girl, bolder is always better.

TOTAL TIME: 15 minutes
ACTIVE TIME: 15 minutes
Serves 4 to 6

Get It
8 to 10 ¼-inch-thick slices French baguette
1 egg yolk, at room temperature

2 teaspoons Dijon mustard

3 tablespoons fresh lemon juice

3 to 4 anchovies (salt-packed or oil-packed), rinsed and chopped to
    a paste

2 large cloves garlic, peeled—1 chopped into a paste and 1 sliced in half

Salt

¾ cup extra-virgin olive oil, plus some for drizzling on the croutons

⅓ cup finely grated Parmigiano-Reggiano cheese

Freshly ground black pepper

2 heads romaine lettuce, torn into large pieces

Go, Girl

◆ Preheat the oven to 375°F.

◆ Begin the croutons: Arrange the baguette slices on a baking sheet.
Toast them in the oven until golden brown, about 8 to 10 minutes.

◆ While the baguette slices are browning, prepare the dressing: In a
blender or small bowl with a whisk, combine the egg yolk, mustard, 2
tablespoons of the lemon juice, anchovies, garlic paste, and a pinch of
salt. With the blender on slow speed, gradually add the ¾ cup olive oil
until it's incorporated. Taste, and add the remaining lemon juice or more
if desired. If the vinaigrette is too thick, thin it with a few teaspoons of
warm water. Transfer the dressing to a bowl and whisk in half of the
cheese. Taste, and season as necessary with salt and pepper.

◆ Remove the toasted baguette slices from the oven and lightly drizzle
them with the remaining olive oil. Rub each slice with the cut garlic clove.

◆ Assemble: In a large salad bowl, dress the lettuce with the vinaigrette.
You may not need all the dressing. Add the remaining cheese, and season

with lots of pepper. Break up the toasted baguette, scatter it over the salad, and serve.

✳ Apple, Endive, and Stilton Salad

In 1996 I stumbled on this recipe in *Gourmet* magazine and went wild for it. Created by Jay Frank, formerly executive chef at the Berkeley Hotel in Richmond, Virginia, and still served by current executive chef Brad Haley, it embodies the perfect party salad: it's elegant, easy, naturally beautiful, and refreshing, and it delivers a lot of bang for minimal bucks. Perfect for spring brunch, summer picnics, and winter dinners, it wows the crowd every time I prepare it. Try this sleek white-and-green wonder and you'll join the ranks of admirers.

TOTAL TIME: 20 minutes
ACTIVE TIME: 20 minutes
Serves 4 to 6

Get It
2 tablespoons white wine vinegar
1 tablespoon red wine vinegar
½ teaspoon Dijon mustard
¾ teaspoon sugar
2 tablespoons extra-virgin olive oil
1 small shallot, minced
⅛ teaspoon salt

Freshly ground black pepper

2 tablespoons unsalted butter

1 cup walnuts, chopped coarse

2 large Belgian endives

2 Granny Smith apples

½ cup Stilton cheese, crumbled

2 tablespoons fresh chopped tarragon leaves

White pepper

Go, Girl

◆ Make the vinaigrette: In a small bowl whisk together the vinegars, mustard, and ¼ teaspoon of the sugar. Add the olive oil, and whisk the vinaigrette until emulsified. Stir in the shallot, salt, and black pepper to taste.

◆ Make candied walnuts: In a small saucepan melt the butter over moderate heat and add the remaining ½ teaspoon sugar and walnuts. Cook the walnuts, stirring, until golden, about 2 minutes. Transfer the walnuts to a bowl.

◆ Cut the endives lengthwise into julienne strips. Quarter and core the apples and cut them into julienne strips.

◆ In a large bowl combine the endives, apples, walnuts, Stilton, tarragon, and vinaigrette, tossing gently, and season with white pepper and more salt to taste.

Deep-Dish Cobb Salad

This very filling classic from L.A.'s bygone Brown Derby restaurant impresses guests with its uncommon sculptural stature. I first saw this salad squared via a mold at L.A.'s very hip Vida restaurant, where playful chef Fred Eric still serves the stacked sensation. Here's my rendition, which you can make as one big Cobb or individual salads depending on what kind of presentation you're after and what kind of molds you use.

TOTAL TIME: 35 minutes
ACTIVE TIME: 35 minutes
Serves 4 as an entree, 6 as a side

Get It
4 eggs
¾ pound bacon
3 medium tomatoes
¾ pound roasted turkey, sliced thick (available from your deli)
2 Hass avocados
½ head romaine lettuce
¼ pound blue cheese
¼ cup red wine vinegar
1 teaspoon Worcestershire sauce
1 teaspoon Dijon mustard
½ teaspoon salt
¼ teaspoon freshly ground black pepper
1 cup extra-virgin olive oil

Go, Girl
◆ Boil the eggs: Put the eggs in a saucepan, cover them completely with water, and bring the water to a boil. Remove the pan from the heat and

let the eggs sit, covered, in the water for 20 minutes. While the eggs are sitting pretty, you can cook the bacon and get chopping.

◆ Cook the bacon: While waiting for the water to boil for the eggs, get the bacon going. I like to cook it under the broiler in a baking tray covered with aluminum foil. You can cook lots of slices at a time this way, and the results tend to be more even. Depending on your oven, it shouldn't take much more than 10 minutes, but unsupervised it can go from just-crunchy to charred in seconds flat, so use a timer and keep an eye on it.

◆ Chop the tomatoes into ½-inch squares, allowing the juice to separate from the solid chunks. Discard the juice; place the tomato chunks in a bowl and set aside.

◆ Chop the turkey into ½-inch squares. Do the same with the avocados. (To get the most out of your avocados, halve them, and then remove the seed by striking it in the center with the blade of a knife and twisting the knife while it's lodged in the seed. Cut a crosshatch pattern through the avocado flesh, and dislodge the pieces by running a knife or your finger along the edge where the skin meets the flesh.)

◆ Now take your knife to the lettuce and chop it into 1-inch squares.

◆ Cool the cooked eggs in cold water, and peel them right under the tap—it's the easiest way to get the shell off. Chop them into ½-inch pieces.

◆ Prepare the salad: Sprinkle the tomato chunks over the bottom of a 9-inch round baking dish (or square, or individual little molds, or any shape mold you want). Add the avocado chunks, making sure they're evenly distributed over the tomatoes. Crumble the blue cheese over the avocado layer, followed by the chopped eggs, again distributing the pieces evenly. Add a layer of bacon, then turkey, and finally the chopped lettuce.

- Gently pack everything down so it fits snugly in the dish, without jumbling the ingredients. Cover the dish tightly with plastic wrap and store it in the fridge until you're ready to serve it.
- Make the dressing: Combine the vinegar, Worcestershire sauce, mustard, salt, pepper, and olive oil, and whisk until it's emulsified.
- When you're ready to serve, remove the salad's plastic wrap, invert a large serving plate over the salad, and while holding the serving dish and the salad mold, turn the dish right side up so that the salad is upside down on top of the dish. Gently tap the bottom of the salad mold so that the salad comes loose and rests on the plate with its shape intact.
- Serve with dressing on the side.

✳ Roasted Beet and Fennel Salad

There are dozens of reasons to become a regular at Bistro Don Giovanni in Napa, California. Along with bartenders Aaron and Ben, who are ever fun to flirt with, there's a festive bar scene, outstanding pastas, and this elegant salad, which I order without fail, since Donna and Giovanni Scala thankfully never take it off the menu. Whip up this colorful and extremely flavorful combination and bring one of Napa Valley's tastiest dining classics to your table.

TOTAL TIME: 1½ hours
ACTIVE TIME: 30 minutes
Serves 4

Get It

1½ pounds medium to large beets, evenly sized (red, golden, chiogga, or all three)

¼ cup plus 1 teaspoon white balsamic vinegar or champagne vinegar

¾ cup plus 2 tablespoons extra-virgin olive oil

½ teaspoon sugar

Salt

4 ounces Roquefort cheese, crumbled

¼ cup champagne vinegar

Freshly ground black pepper

1 fennel bulb, halved and sliced into ⅛-inch-thick pieces

1 pound haricots verts (or green beans, if you can't find them), cleaned and blanched until just tender

¼ head radicchio, cut into fine julienne (optional)

1 avocado, ripe but not too soft, cut into ½-inch cubes

1 bunch chives, minced fine

Go, Girl

◆ Preheat the oven to 375°F.

◆ Roast the beets: Wash the beets and dry them with a towel. In a bowl toss them with ¼ cup balsamic and 2 tablespoons olive oil. Place the beets and the vinegar-oil mixture in a baking dish or pan and roast the beets in the oven until they're tender when pierced with a toothpick or skewer, about 45 minutes to an hour.

◆ Let the beets cool slightly; peel and dice them while they're still warm. Sprinkle the beets with the sugar, salt to taste, and the remaining 1 teaspoon balsamic, and set them aside to cool. Once the beets have cooled, chop them into ¾-inch cubes.

◆ Prepare the Roquefort vinaigrette: Place half the Roquefort and the champagne vinegar in a bowl and sprinkle with salt and pepper. Slowly whisk in the remaining ¾ cup olive oil until emulsified.

◆ Assemble the salad: Place the beets, fennel, haricots verts, and radicchio in a bowl. Sprinkle with salt and pepper. Add half of the vinaigrette and toss gently. Add more dressing if it's too dry.

◆ Scoop the salad onto four plates or a serving platter. Top with the avocado and remaining Roquefort. Sprinkle with chives and serve.

✳

ONE WEEKEND WHEN I was working as a cook at a touchy-feely California retreat, someone asked me to make a salami and turkey sandwich without bread. Since I didn't have any big leafy greens to hold the sandwich together, I diced the meat and some lettuce and tomatoes and mixed it with mustard and mayonnaise. My "meat salad" was born. It's not something I would serve to someone who didn't ask specifically for it, but I have to admit that it tasted surprisingly good. More important, it was a great reminder that salads always look amazing when everything's chopped and tossed together. Next time you have a bunch of seemingly boring salad ingredients (even something as simple as a head of butter lettuce and a tomato), take a knife to them, chop them small, mix them in a pretty bowl, drizzle with dressing, and get a fresh perspective.

7

Elegant Entrees

WHENEVER I'M FEELING critical of my cooking, I tell myself this story. On Valentine's Day when I was seven years old, word spread through school that Mark, a cute boy in my class, had distributed homemade sugar cookies in the cubbies of girls he liked. I raced to my cubby with great anticipation and was relieved to find a bag waiting for me. Simultaneously, other girls discovered they were also fortunate recipients. I could see that in their Baggies were perfect heart-shaped sugar cookies. But when I looked into my Baggie, my heart sank. Mine were dented, funky, misshapen hearts, the rejects with lumpy sides and burned, thin edges. All day I fumed. I was the reject-cookie girl. I hated Mark. When school got out, I ran into his mother in the parking lot. "Did you like your cookies?" she asked. I probably grimaced, because she bent down, put her hand on my shoulder, and told me the thing that made me understand why all homemade food is wonderful even when it's not. "You know, the cookies you got were the ones Mark made himself," she said. I melted like butter. My heart grew bigger than all the cookies combined. With my fresh perspective, those previously defective cookies were the most beautiful things

I'd ever seen, and I knew I was lucky to receive them. I've never forgotten that anything made for me by someone else is a gift in itself. If you're ever feeling down on your culinary prowess, remember that a special meal is not about the perfection of the sea bass, but about the love you put into it.

*

These main courses are easy, glamorous, and more seductive than a shirtless Brad Pitt (OK, almost). Turn to them when you want stunning homemade feasts in a flash. Straight from some of the nation's most talented chefs and from my secret recipe book, most of these Elegant Entrees require only minutes to prepare. Others demand a little more planning and time. But even those that need to sit and simmer don't require that a busy go-girl baby-sit them. They're categorized into groups of pasta, fish, fowl, and meat and subcategorized from easiest to most time-consuming. Select your supper superstar, put on some sizzling tunes and an apron, and go, girl.

Once you've chosen your entree, consider whether it needs a sexy sidekick or can hold its own. Pastas need nothing more than a starter salad, a good loaf of crusty bread, and an olive oil dipping sauce, but for almost everything else you'll want to add a vegetable, starch (think rice, potatoes, or polenta), or both. Pair your main course with the perfect sidekick, which you'll find in the following chapter.

Hiro's Heroic Tomato Sauce

This recipe is one reason why Japanese chef Hiro Sone is my hero. The culinary force behind Terra, one of the top restaurants in Napa Valley, California, Hiro is a master in Japanese, French, and Italian cuisine. He's also a closet rocker and the brain behind this supersimple and excellent sauce. It may seem odd, but a V-8–based pasta sauce makes perfect sense. Recipes often require that vegetable flavors be simmered over time into the sauce, but with Hiro's Heroic there's no need to wait or work hard. Even before I agreed to accompany him to a Scorpions and Deep Purple concert (much to the relief of his wife and chef, Lissa Doumani, who wanted none of it), he sent me his easy, customizable, and unbelievably delicious secret pasta sauce recipe with a note that read, "I use this tomato sauce for my pasta at home all the time. After I plate it, I drizzle good extra-virgin olive oil over the pasta." Taste for yourself why this straight-up effortless sauce is pure genius.

TOTAL TIME: 10 to 15 minutes
ACTIVE TIME: 5 minutes
Serves 4

Get It
¼ cup extra-virgin olive oil
4 teaspoons chopped garlic
2 12-ounce cans V-8 juice
Salt and freshly ground black pepper

Go, Girl

◆ Heat the olive oil and garlic in a saucepan over medium heat. Gently shake the pan to caramelize the garlic evenly.

◆ The minute you see the garlic get some color, remove the pan from the heat and add the V-8.

◆ Put the pan back on the heat, bring the juice to a boil, season with salt and pepper, and let it simmer until it's your preferred consistency.

◆ Serve over pasta.

Variations

For variety, Hiro suggests you add any of the following:

Red chili flakes—spice it up!

Capers, olives, and anchovy—à la puttanesca. (Lissa likes to add a can of tuna to the puttanesca sauce.)

Saffron and shrimp—fisherman style.

White wine and clams—with linguine.

Basil—classic!

Cream—romantic pink color.

Anything you want—it's not his responsibility.

✳ Angel Hair Pasta with Smoked Salmon and Golden Caviar

I first turned to this recipe in *The Wolfgang Puck Cookbook* (Random House, 1996) when I was twenty-three and wanted to impress my boss, who was coming over for dinner. Wolfgang makes his own pasta and serves small portions as an appetizer for four people. But this last-minute go-girl used packaged pasta and found the recipe makes a nice main course for two. Aside from boiling water, it took no more than ten minutes and required virtually no skills on my part, but it was so delicate, flavorful, and luxurious that it made me seem like a culinary genius. Wolfgang's recipe clued me in to a simple secret of cream sauces: they're intrinsically opulent and absurdly easy. Start with cream, add a few other ingredients, toss it with al dente pasta (follow the package directions and don't overcook it!), and—Ta-da!—you've masterminded a rich and decadent feast. It's not for those who are lactose intolerant or overly weight conscious, but for go-girls who know the merits of casting calorie cares to the wind, there are few easier ways to go.

TOTAL TIME: 15 minutes
ACTIVE TIME: 10 minutes
Serves 2

Get It
1 tablespoon extra-virgin olive oil
1 cup heavy cream
Freshly ground white pepper
Salt
¼ pound dried angel hair pasta
6 ounces smoked salmon, julienned
4 ounces golden caviar (Unlike many other caviars, this one is extremely
    affordable at around $5 per ounce.)
2 tablespoons minced chives or chervil leaves

Go, Girl

◆ Bring a large pot of water and the olive oil to a boil.

◆ Pour the cream into a large skillet. Add the pepper. Just before cooking the pasta, bring the cream to a boil and then remove the skillet from the heat.

◆ Add a little salt to the boiling water, and then add the pasta and cook it until al dente ("to the tooth" in Italian, or not too soft and still a bit firm).

◆ Rinse the pasta quickly under hot water and drain it.

◆ Toss the pasta and the salmon with the hot cream in the skillet, and heat the mixture through.

◆ Stir in half the caviar and correct the seasonings.

◆ Divide the pasta among two warm plates, and garnish each serving with the remaining caviar and a light sprinkling of the chives or chervil.

Party Girl's Cream Sauce Variations

Stick with the olive oil, cream, white pepper, and salt, skip the other ingredients, and go for it with:

Vodka Pasta: Omit the white pepper and add a bit of tomato puree, vodka, minced onion, tomatoes, and salt and pepper to taste, with penne.

Fettuccine Alfredo: Add grated Parmesan or Swiss cheese, with fettuccine.

Fettuccine Carbonara: Add prosciutto or cooked bacon, butter, and Parmesan, with fettuccine.

Cajun Pasta: Add cubed chicken, onion powder, garlic powder, cayenne, thyme, black pepper, oregano, and paprika, with fettuccine.

Fettuccine with Swiss Chard, Currants, Walnuts, and Brown Butter

This gorgeous vegetarian recipe is adapted from *Field of Greens* (Bantam Doubleday Dell Publishers, 1993), a wonderful vegetarian cookbook by Annie Somerville, the chef behind San Francisco's top vegetarian restaurant, Greens. I serve it even to meat lovers, who quickly find themselves enamored with this noncarnivorous fettuccine feast. I agree with Annie, who says the pasta's "perfect for a midwinter meal." She adds, "The flavors are full and rich—hearty sautéed chard, crunchy walnuts, and the sweetness of currants and golden raisins. The brown butter coats the pasta, and its warm, nutty flavor permeates the dish." Now that your mouth is watering, get to it with either fettuccine or penne.

TOTAL TIME: 40 minutes

ACTIVE TIME: 30 minutes

Serves 2 to 4

Get It

½ pound unsalted butter

1 tablespoon dried currants

2 tablespoons golden raisins

1 bunch red or green Swiss chard (about 8 cups packed leaves)

1 tablespoon light olive oil

½ medium-size red onion, sliced thin (about 1 cup)

1½ teaspoons salt plus extra for seasoning

Freshly ground black pepper

2 cloves garlic, peeled and chopped fine

¼ pound dried fettuccine

⅓ cup walnut pieces, toasted (see Toasted Nuts in Chapter 5)

Freshly grated Parmesan cheese

Go, Girl

◆ Melt the butter in a small saucepan over low heat. As the butter gently simmers, the butterfat and milk solids will separate. The solids will settle to the bottom, coloring the butter as it cooks. When the butter turns a rich amber color, in about 8 to 10 minutes, remove the pan from the heat. Line a fine-mesh strainer with a paper towel or cheesecloth and pour the

PERFECT PASTA

You should know a few keys to cooking perfect pasta. First, use a big pot filled with lots of water, about 2 quarts per half pound of dry pasta. When the water boils, add a tablespoon of salt before you add the pasta. Stir the pasta to keep it from sticking. Cook it for the time indicated on the package, but also test it by taking a bite. If it's got just a touch of resistance, or firmness, it's time to get your pasta out of the hot water. Strain it quickly, transfer the pasta to a pan or pot with the sauce, combine over medium-high heat, and serve immediately. You can also remove the pasta from the water while it's still a little too firm, drain it, toss it with a little olive oil to make sure it doesn't stick together, set it aside until you're ready to serve, and then heat it with the sauce. This tactic is especially good if you want to prepare the pasta in advance.

butter through it, straining out the solids. Keep the strained butter warm over low heat.

◆ Set a large pot of water to boil.

◆ Meanwhile, plump the currants and raisins by placing them in a small bowl and covering them with ¼ cup hot water.

◆ Trim the stems from the chard, and slice across the leaves to make 2-inch-wide ribbons.

◆ Heat the olive oil in a large sauté pan; add the onion, ¼ teaspoon of the salt, and a few pinches of pepper. Sauté over medium heat for about 5 minutes, until the onion softens and begins to release its juices. Add the garlic, chard, and another ¼ teaspoon of the salt. Sauté for 4 to 5 minutes, until the chard is just barely tender, and then reduce the heat to low.

◆ When the water boils, add the remaining 1 teaspoon salt to the pot. Add the fettuccine to the boiling water, timing it to finish cooking with the chard. (The chard should be very tender but not overcooked when the pasta is done.) When the pasta is just tender, drain it immediately in a colander, shake off the excess water, and add it to the onions and chard, along with the plumped fruit, walnuts, and brown butter. Toss together and season with salt and pepper to taste. Serve with Parmesan.

✳ Hiro's Mother Sauce
. . . .

If elegant, light, healthy fare is on your menu, you've found heaven with chef Hiro Sone's Mother Sauce. This outstanding marinade recipe from Terra in Napa Valley is extremely versatile and adds Japanese flavor to everything from stir-fried vegetables and braised meats to grilled or broiled seafood, and roasted, sautéed, or grilled meats. (See "Hiro's Variations" for cooking details.) Terra is famous for its Mother Sauce–

HIRO'S VARIATIONS

Hiro comes to the party-girl rescue with myriad ways to add gorgeous Japanese flavor to your feast. Follow his lead:

- Marinate fish for 2 to 6 hours. Think black cod, salmon, or a halibut fillet. Then broil the fish in a broiler-safe baking dish for about 8 minutes. Or sauté or grill it. You can also marinate meats such as chicken breasts, pork chops, ribs, and steak, which can then be grilled, sautéed, or roasted to your liking. Marinated tofu can be sautéed.
- In a pan, stir-fry your favorite vegetables, mushrooms, meat, or a mix of everything with oil, and then season with this sauce to taste.
- Braise (i.e., cook covered over low heat) meat or vegetables in this sauce mixed with water: Place the meat in a pot, cover it with water, and bring the water to a boil. Skim and discard any fat or foam, and add sauce to taste. Braise beef short ribs 2½ hours, pork shoulder 2 hours, and duck legs 1½ hours. Before the meat is finished cooking, add vegetables. Hiro likes potatoes, green beans, mushrooms, and carrots. Transfer the cooked meat and veggies to a plate, add a little of the sauce, and serve with steamed rice or noodles.
- For a miniature Peking duck, marinate quail (bone-in) for 6 hours, pat them dry, and then deep-fry in vegetable oil at 350°F (think reasonably high heat) for 4 to 5 minutes. You can also broil the birds for around 7 minutes.

marinated cod (previously sea bass, before it became an endangered no-no), and I've garnered rave reviews among food-professional friends for serving fish that soaked in the sauce before being broiled. You'll have to hit an Asian market for a few of the ingredients, but trust me: it's worth the detour. Also, make extra! Covered and refrigerated, the sauce keeps up to a month.

TOTAL TIME: Depends on what you use it for (see "Hiro's Variations")
ACTIVE TIME: 5 minutes
Serves 4

Get It
½ cup mirin
½ cup soy sauce
¼ cup sugar
¼ teaspoon grated garlic
¼ teaspoon grated ginger

Go, Girl
◆ Whisk all the ingredients in a mixing bowl, cover, and refrigerate.

✳ Two-Second Teriyaki-Style Salmon

OK. It takes more than two seconds, but this may be the easiest thing I've ever made, and whenever I serve it, guests beg for the recipe. So, here it is, for your effortless-eating pleasure. In this recipe you serve the salmon on a bed of greens. You can also skip the greens and add Rice along with Sautéed Asparagus (both in Chapter 8), drizzled with the cooked marinade.

TOTAL TIME: 2 hours, 10 minutes

ACTIVE TIME: 15 minutes

Serves 4

Get It

½ cup brown sugar

½ cup soy sauce

4 ⅓-pound salmon fillets

1 tablespoon olive oil

8 cups spinach

½ cup toasted walnut pieces (optional; see Toasted Nuts in Chapter 5)

Go, Girl

◆ In a bowl mix the brown sugar and soy sauce until all the sugar has dissolved.

◆ Marinate the salmon—skin-side up, provided you bought it with the skin still on—in the sauce, covered with a lid or plastic wrap and refrigerated, for 2 to 8 hours.

◆ In a pan, heat the oil over a moderate flame and add the fish skin-side down, reserving the marinade.

◆ Cook the salmon for about 4 to 5 minutes on each side (depending on the thickness), or until the outside is golden brown and crisp and the center looks pink but not completely cooked (look at the sides while the fish is cooking to check for doneness). If the skin sticks to the pan (it might), slough it off with a spatula and throw it away.

◆ Fish will continue to cook after you've removed the pan from the flame, so if you're like me and you prefer salmon medium rare to medium, add approximately half of the marinade now, cook for 2 more minutes, and take the pan off of the stove. Want it well done? Cook the fish for a few more minutes before adding the marinade. (The marinade will burn if it's kept for too long at high heat, so don't add it until the last minute and keep the flame low.) Set the cooked fish aside, reserving the marinade.

◆ In a bowl combine the spinach, walnuts, and reserved marinade. Distribute the spinach mixture among your dinner plates, and top with teriyaki-glazed salmon.

Sexy Mixed Seafood

While I was living in L.A., caterer Phillip Weingarten's house was my second home. One summer I did almost nothing but float in his pool while listening to the *Bulworth* soundtrack and *Big Calm* by Morcheeba. (OK, maybe I worked a little, too.) An excellent party boy himself, Phillip never lets guests go hungry and always serves food with style. One of my fondest meal memories from that supreme summer is this foil-wrapped seafood surprise, which takes mere minutes of prep and is flexible because you can customize the seafood by adding or subtracting whatever you like. Serve it with crusty bread and either Orzo, Couscous, or Potatoes with Parsley (all in Chapter 8).

TOTAL TIME: 40 minutes
ACTIVE TIME: 20 minutes
Serves 4

Get It

4 tablespoons (½ stick) unsalted butter, at room temperature

8 medium shrimp, unpeeled

4 jumbo scallops

8 mussels

8 clams

4 ⅓- to ½-pound halibut or salmon fillets (they should be about as thick
   as your scallops)

1 teaspoon salt

Freshly ground black pepper

1 cup chopped tomato (optional)

4 teaspoons fresh minced thyme

4 teaspoons minced chives (optional)

4 teaspoons fresh minced parsley

3 lemons

1 cup white wine

Go, Girl

◆ Preheat the oven to 425°F.

◆ Spread four 18″ × 12″ pieces of heavy-duty aluminum foil on a flat surface with the shiny side facing down. Coat the top of each sheet with 1
tablespoon butter.

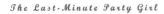

◆ Prepare a foil pocket: Fold the foil in half toward you so that the folded sheet measures 9″ × 12″. Starting on the left side, make a ¼-inch fold. Fold toward the middle, as if you're folding the end of a lunch bag, only much smaller and tighter. Repeat at least four times, making the folds as tight as possible. Do the same on the right side. Now you should have a pocket with one side still open. Repeat with the other three sheets, or if you're lazy buy Reynolds Wrap Hot Bags Foil Bags.

◆ Pull the legs off the shrimp, leaving the shell on and intact.

◆ Distribute the shrimp, scallops, mussels, clams, and halibut evenly inside the four foil pockets.

◆ Season each with ¼ teaspoon salt and a little pepper.

◆ Add ¼ cup tomato and 1 teaspoon thyme, chives, and parsley to each foil pocket.

◆ Cut two of the lemons in half and the other into eight wheels (thin slices widthwise).

◆ Squeeze half a lemon over each portion, and place two lemon wheels inside each pocket.

◆ Now tilt each pocket with its mouth upward and pour in ¼ cup white wine; then carefully seal the pocket by folding the open side up tightly like the others. The idea here is to keep all the liquid and moisture in the foil while the seafood cooks.

◆ Put your seafood pockets on a baking sheet, shove it in the oven, and bake for 15 to 20 minutes, depending on the thickness of your seafood.

◆ Serve your seafood surprise in the foil bags. Cut a little *X* in the top so an aromatic steam tempts guests to pull their bags apart and discover what's inside. Have a bowl nearby for discarding the foil.

Grilled Swordfish with Worcestershire Vinaigrette and Roasted Vegetables

Michael Mina became a culinary superstar as the executive chef behind the spectacular seafood at Aqua restaurant in San Francisco and Vegas. He created this home-chef-friendly feast, which rocks because it's healthy and easy enough for every day but also sexy enough to serve to your most discerning dinner guests.

TOTAL TIME: 45 minutes

ACTIVE TIME: 30 minutes

Serves 4

Get It

4 new potatoes, halved

8 baby beets

12 baby carrots, peeled

8 shiitake mushrooms, stems removed

8 shallots, peeled and halved

1 cup extra-virgin olive oil

Salt and freshly ground black pepper

¼ cup Worcestershire sauce

½ sprig of rosemary, chopped

2 tablespoons chopped chives

1 small clove garlic, peeled and minced

1½ teaspoons balsamic vinegar

1½ teaspoons lemon juice

4 6-ounce pieces of swordfish

½ pound arugula

1 pound red and yellow cherry tomatoes

Go, Girl

♦ Preheat the oven to 375°F.

♦ Heat an iron skillet or other ovenproof pan in the oven. Keeping the potatoes, beets, carrots, mushrooms, and shallots separate, toss each in approximately 1 tablespoon of the olive oil, and season with salt and pepper. Place the vegetables, still in their separate groups, in the heated skillet and roast them until tender, about 30 minutes.

♦ Meanwhile, make the vinaigrette: Mix the Worcestershire sauce, rosemary, chives, garlic, balsamic, lemon juice, and ½ cup of the remaining olive oil, adding salt and pepper to taste. Set it aside.

♦ Season the swordfish with salt and pepper. Coat a grill or pan with 2 teaspoons of the remaining olive oil, and brown the fish over medium heat, about 1 to 2 minutes on each side.

♦ Transfer the fish to a baking dish and continue cooking it in the oven until medium rare, about 5 to 10 minutes depending on the thickness of the fish. (If you're not sure if the fish is cooked, make a small incision to check.)

♦ When you remove the vegetables from the oven, let them cool enough that they can be handled, and peel the beets with a vegetable peeler.

♦ Reheat the vegetables just before you're ready to serve.

♦ Coat a large sauté pan with the remaining 1 tablespoon olive oil, and sauté the arugula and tomatoes until the greens start to wilt, about 4 minutes.

- ◆ Mix the greens with the hot vegetables.
- ◆ Divide the mixture among your serving plates, place the swordfish atop the vegetables, pour vinaigrette over each portion, and serve.

Quiche Lorraine

Contrary to popular belief, most men do like quiche. Likewise your gal pals. A fabulous brunch or lunch item in a flaky pastry package, this egg-based beauty is also ideal for large parties. I've hosted a gaggle of twenty-five gals with nothing more than five quiches, a big salad, store-bought breakfast pastries, and bubbly. It's just as easy to make five as it is one—and you can make vegetarian and meat variations (details follow). Note: If you want a crisper crust, partially bake the piecrust first, following the directions on the package.

TOTAL TIME: 1 hour
ACTIVE TIME: 20 minutes
Serves 6 to 8

Get It
6 slices bacon
4 eggs
2 cups heavy cream or a mix of cream and milk
Salt
1 store-bought piecrust
½ cup Gruyère cheese, chopped into chunks

Go, Girl

◆ Preheat the oven to 375°F.

◆ Cook the bacon by either frying it in a pan over medium heat or putting it on a baking sheet and giving it a few minutes under the broiler.

EGG CENTRIC

If perhaps your party rocked all night and rolled into the next morning, and you're trashed but you need to impress that surprise slumber-party guest, make an easy egg breakfast. My personal favorite is an instant soufflé-style scramble, which is possible only if you have an espresso machine: Scramble an egg in a tall thick glass, add a teaspoon of water, and start your espresso machine's steamer. Steam the egg as though you are steaming milk, and 15 seconds later you've got the world's fluffiest scramble. Place it in the center of a plate, wipe away any residual liquid, top it with a sprig of parsley and a pinch of salt, and you're Backseat Betty Crocker. (Toss in toast with jam if you've got it.) Another option is to take a slice of white bread and cut a silver-dollar-size hole in the middle (or use a cute-shaped cookie cutter). Throw a teaspoon of butter in a sauté pan over medium heat, brown the bread on one side, add another teaspoon of butter, and flip the bread. While the second side is browning, carefully crack an egg into the bread hole. Cook at medium heat for 3 minutes, carefully flip the toast with the egg, cook for 3 more minutes, remove from heat, and serve. The egg should be over-easy in the middle. If you prefer harder yolks, cook longer. Now go back to bed.

The bacon should be rather floppy, not crispy. When the bacon is cool, cut each piece in half.

◆ Whisk the eggs and cream together until well combined. Add a generous pinch of salt.

◆ Spread the bacon out on the bottom of the piecrust, sprinkle the cheese evenly over the bacon, and carefully add the egg mixture.

◆ Cook the quiche in the middle of the oven for 30 to 40 minutes, or until it is just firm and doesn't seem runny in the middle.

◆ Let it cool slightly and serve.

Variations

Vegetable Quiche: Add steamed broccoli or spinach, or both, to the egg mix and substitute Swiss cheese for the Gruyère.

Mushroom Quiche: Sauté chopped mushrooms in butter over medium heat until their liquid has evaporated and they're nice and brown. Add them to the egg mix with your choice of cheese.

Caramelized Onion Quiche: Substitute sautéed sliced onions for the mushrooms in the preceding variation, with either Gruyère or Swiss cheese.

Chicken Roulades

I adore this recipe because it's seriously last-minute, extremely inexpensive, and forgiving if you forget it in the oven. Basically, this roulade (French for a meat roll and pronounced "roo-LAHD") is nothing more than boned, rolled-up chicken thighs. But carved into little pinwheels, they're a pretty package of inherently juicy chicken with crunchy-crisp skin. You can serve them atop leafy greens as a lunch entree or cram 'em with any fillings that feed your dinnertime fantasy. I've stuffed my thighs—literally and figuratively—with everything from sun-dried tomatoes, pine nuts, and goat cheese to Thai marinade and fresh basil and served them with flavored rice (the store-bought stuff) and Sautéed Asparagus (see Chapter 8).

TOTAL TIME: 45 minutes
ACTIVE TIME: 10 minutes
Serves 4

Get It

8 chicken thighs (boned, if you're lazy and you have a good butcher)
Seasoning—any salt-based seasoning mix will do, or go for a hearty
    sprinkle of coriander, paprika, salt, and pepper

Go, Girl

◆ Preheat the oven to 400°F.

◆ If the chicken thighs aren't boned, carefully cut the meat away from the bone in one piece, doing your best to leave none behind. Trim off all visible fat (not the skin, but the soft yellowish stuff stuck within sections of the meat).

◆ Lay the chicken skin-side down, and season the strips with spices. (If you're stuffing the rolls with anything, now's the time to do it: add a thin layer on top of the meat.)

- Roll up each boneless chicken thigh like a sleeping bag and season the outer (skin) side.
- Bake the chicken in the upper section of the oven for a half hour, or until the skin is crisp. If the skin's not cooperating, crank up the heat at the last minute and give it a quick broil.
- Remove the chicken from the oven and let it cool slightly. Cut off and discard the uncrisp skin on the underside of the roulades, and then slice each widthwise so that the centers have a cinnamon-bun-like swirl. Serve the roulades with your desired accompaniments. (Think atop a salad or with store-bought couscous and veggies.)

Whole Roasted Chicken and Roasted Vegetables

The beauty of roasting a whole chicken is that prep takes about ten minutes, and thirty minutes after you throw it in the oven, savory aromas fill the kitchen and announce that a freshly made feast is on the way. It also looks beautiful—brown-skinned and sitting pretty amid veggies that have been bathing in the juices—and is easily a meal for four, since the side dishes roast right alongside the bird. Cutting the chicken from the bone is the most challenging part, but even if you mangle the meat, it's no matter. The flavor more than makes up for it.

TOTAL TIME: 2 hours
ACTIVE TIME: 15 minutes
Serves 4

Get It

1 4-pound chicken

2 tablespoons unsalted butter, at room temperature

Salt and freshly ground black pepper

½ lemon, sliced

8 cloves garlic, peeled, plus 3 cloves peeled and mashed

1 teaspoon chopped rosemary

4 cups mixed carrots, onions, and potatoes, chopped into 1-inch pieces

2 tablespoons extra-virgin olive oil

Go, Girl

◆ Preheat the oven to 425°F.

◆ Discard any giblets if they were included in your chicken.

◆ Rinse the chicken under hot water, and dry it with paper towels. Rub the butter over the outside of the bird, and generously salt the chicken inside and out.

◆ Insert a pinch or two of pepper and the lemon slices in the cavity, squeezing the slices to release some of the juice.

◆ Rub the mashed garlic and rosemary under the skin on the breast side.

◆ In a bowl toss the vegetables and the garlic cloves in the olive oil, and then transfer them to a roasting pan.

◆ Arrange the chicken breast-side up on a roasting rack over the vegetables. If you don't have a roasting rack, don't sweat it: just prop the chicken up on the veggies and know that your side dish will be a little mashed (call it "rustic") when you dish it up. If you've got twine, tie the legs together to close up the bird's cavity. If not, don't worry about it.

◆ Place the chicken in the bottom half of the oven; after 10 minutes, lower the heat to 350°F and continue roasting until done, approximately 1¾ hours total.

◆ Let the chicken rest for at least 10 minutes before carving.

◆ Serve the whole thing—chicken, veggies, pan juices, and all—on a serving tray.

Variations

Oven-Barbecued Chicken with Roasted Veggies: Skip the salt, lemon, garlic, rosemary, and onions; smear barbecue sauce over the bird before cooking.

Lemon Chicken: Forget the garlic and rosemary; squeeze half a lemon over the chicken, and add pepper to the outside of the bird.

Chicken and Rice: Omit the veggies, and use the juices to flavor white rice.

Sautéed Quail with Roasted Red Onion Panzanella

Chef Craig Stoll is famous in food and magazine circles for his Italian restaurant Delfina in San Francisco. He's also the generous creator of this ridiculously good dish. Even if you never make it to his Mission District neighborhood hot spot, you'll understand his allure if you try this recipe. I literally jumped up and down when I first made the bread salad, which soaks up the accompanying dressing and releases it into your mouth in gorgeous flavor bursts. Don't hesitate! Just try it—especially when you want to impress friends. Trust me: it's easier than it looks. Delfina usually serves the bread salad as an accompaniment to quail or squab roasted in the wood-fired oven, but it makes a fine partner to chicken and other meats as well. FYI, *panzanella* is an Italian bread salad typically made with tomatoes and cucumber. Since tomato season is brief, Craig developed this bread salad that can be made year-round.

TOTAL TIME: 50 minutes

ACTIVE TIME: 30 minutes

Serves 4

Get It

1 red onion

½ cup extra-virgin olive oil

¼ cup balsamic vinegar

Kosher salt

Freshly ground black pepper

1 loaf Italian bread (think crusty rustic loaf; any bakery or grocery store with a good fresh bread selection should have it)

6 semiboneless quail (with the rib cage removed but the leg and thighbone left in) or 3 boneless chicken breasts

6 tablespoons unsalted butter, at room temperature

½ cup chicken stock (available at any supermarket)

1 tablespoon pine nuts

1 teaspoon chopped fresh thyme

2 cups arugula or dandelion greens

7 cherry tomatoes, halved (optional)

For the sherry wine vinaigrette:
⅛ cup sherry wine vinegar
¼ teaspoon finely chopped shallot
Salt and freshly ground black pepper
⅜ cup extra-virgin olive oil

Go, Girl

◆ Roast the onion: Cut the onion lengthwise, through the root, into quarters or sixths, depending on the size. Toss the pieces in a bowl with ¼ cup of the olive oil, the balsamic, and salt and pepper to taste. Lay the onion pieces on a sheet pan and roast at 350°F for about 25 minutes; turn the pieces over and roast for another 15 to 20 minutes. The onion should be lightly browned on the outside and soft and creamy inside.

◆ When the onion is done cooking, let the pieces cool and then cut off the roots, allowing the sections to fall apart into individual "petals." Discard the skin. Combine the onion with any residual cooking juices in a nonreactive bowl (either glass or high-quality stainless steel) and set it aside.

◆ While the onion is cooking, begin the bread salad: Cut the crusts off of the bread with a bread knife and then tear the loaf by hand into 1-inch pieces. In a stainless steel bowl toss the bread with a pinch of salt and the remaining ¼ cup of olive oil. Spread the bread out on a sheet pan and bake at 350°F for about 5 minutes, or until lightly browned.

◆ Make the vinaigrette: Combine the vinegar and shallot in a nonreactive bowl. Season with salt and pepper and allow the shallot to soak in the vinegar for 10 minutes. Whisk in the olive oil a little at a time until emulsified. Set the vinaigrette aside.

◆ Prepare the quail: Cut the wing tips off of the quail. "Butterfly" the quail by cutting them along the back and spread them open on the counter, skin-side down. Season the inside lightly with salt and pepper, and then flip them over and season the skin side. Heat a large sauté pan over a high flame until it begins to smoke. Put the butter in the pan and tilt the pan as the butter begins to melt. Add the quail, skin-side down, and spread them out flat. If you don't have a pan big enough, use two pans at once or cook the quail in batches. Don't crowd the pan, or the quail will steam instead of browning. Continue to cook over high heat until the quail are sizzling. Lift each quail up with tongs and tilt the pan to make sure there is sufficient butter underneath. Turn the heat down a little, but keep it high enough to brown the skin side well. When the skin side is deep brown and crispy, flip the quail over for a brief moment, and then remove them from the pan. You want the quail just cooked through, not well done. (If you're substituting chicken, cook it longer, until it's cooked through, about 15 to 20 minutes.)

◆ Finish the bread salad: Bring the poultry stock to a boil in a saucepan and continue boiling until the liquid is reduced by half, so that about ¼ cup of stock remains. Place the toasted bread in a large stainless steel bowl and season it with salt and pepper. Add 3 tablespoons of the vinaigrette and then the hot stock. Toss the ingredients together so that the bread absorbs the liquids. Toss in the roasted onion, pine nuts, thyme, greens, and tomatoes.

◆ Serve: Lay the quail on the counter, skin-side down, and cut each in half. Arrange the quail with the bread salad, allowing three half birds per person.

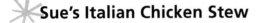

Sue's Italian Chicken Stew

Aside from love, my godmother, Sue Diodati, has given me two very important things in my life. One was a consolation bottle of champagne when I was a teenager grounded on New Year's Eve. The other is this recipe. It's an adaptation of the rabbit stew made by her father, Joe, who learned it from his mother while growing up in the small town of Marlia, Italy, in the 1910s. Joe's family was poor. Their meals consisted of whatever they hunted and grew. But as the only son, who liked to help in the kitchen, he became wealthy with a culinary repertoire that he brought to the States and shared with his own family. It's impossible not to be enamored by this soul-satisfying dish that's rich in flavor and family history. Sue serves it with soft Polenta (see Chapter 8) or saffron rice (two packages of Mahatma ready-made rice does the trick) and people she loves. Lucky me, and by association lucky you. *Bon appetito!*

TOTAL TIME: 1 hour
ACTIVE TIME: 40 minutes
Serves 4

Get It

1 chicken cut into pieces by your local butcher, or a mix of legs, thighs, and wings (for Joe's Rabbit, substitute 1 2½- to 3-pound rabbit, washed and chopped into pieces by your butcher)

3 cloves garlic, peeled and sliced

¼ cup extra-virgin olive oil

1 cup whole bitter olives, pits included (think black Mediterranean or kalamata)

The easiest way to get rosemary needles off of the stem is to hold the top of the rosemary branch with one hand and with your other hand run pinched fingers from the top of the branch to the bottom, pulling the needles away from the stem as you go-girl.

3 chopped fresh sage leaves

1 to 4 tablespoons chopped fresh rosemary needles (amount depends on
    how much you like rosemary; see the accompanying tip on "pinching"
    the needles)

¼ cup chopped fresh thyme

¼ cup chopped fresh parsley

¾ cup dry white wine

¾ cup chicken broth

8 ounces tomato sauce

Go, Girl

◆ In a large skillet or sauté pan brown the meat and garlic in olive oil over medium heat. When both sides of the meat are browned, add the olives and cook for 6 minutes.

◆ Stir in the sage, rosemary, thyme, and parsley and cook until the herbs are lightly brown.

◆ Add the wine, boil for a few minutes, and then reduce the heat to a simmer.

◆ In a separate pot bring the chicken broth to a boil, and then transfer it to the pan of simmering meat and boil for 10 minutes.

- ◆ Add the tomato sauce and 4 ounces of water and let the stew simmer for 30 minutes, or until it thickens to a consistency you like.
- ◆ Serve it in the pot and let your guests dig in.

Painless Pan-Fried Steak with Red Wine Sauce

I first learned how easy it is to make a great steak on the stove top from my mother, who learned it from *Mastering the Art of French Cooking* by Julia Child, Louisette Bertholle, and Simone Beck (Alfred A. Knopf, Inc., 1961). Impress your meat-and-potatoes man or treat yourself with this adaptation of Child's superbly simple carnivorous delight, which can be taken over the top with Potato Gratin or Mashed Potatoes (both in Chapter 8).

TOTAL TIME: 20 minutes
ACTIVE TIME: 20 minutes
Serves 2

Get It
2 steaks (cut and size are your preference, but ideally at least 1½ inches thick)
Salt and freshly ground black pepper
2 tablespoons butter
1 tablespoon extra-virgin olive oil
1 tablespoon chopped shallot (optional)
⅓ cup red wine
1 teaspoon minced parsley (optional)

PRETTY PEPPER

....

If you want to add a pretty pepper touch to your steak or any other dish, consider a trick I spied at The French Laundry, one of the world's most revered restaurants. Inside the discreet dining room in Yountville, California, chef-owner Thomas Keller creates edible works of art that justify forking over around $250 for a nine-course tasting menu and beautifully paired wines. Most of Thomas's mastery is far too detailed for the last-minute partyer, but you can add a sprinkle of French Laundry flair to dinner: Break out your pepper mill, leave an empty spot on each dinner plate, and just before serving, place the mill directly on the plate, hold it firmly in place, and grind the pepper. Carefully remove the grinder and you should have a pepper circle. How cool is that?

Go, Girl

◆ Season the steaks with salt and pepper.

◆ In a large, heavy skillet heat 1 tablespoon of the butter and the olive oil over a medium-high flame for about 2 minutes, or until the butter stops foaming.

◆ Add the steaks, cooking for about 5 minutes on one side and 3 minutes on the other—longer if you like your steaks medium or well done. (Cut into it if you can't tell if it's cooked to your liking.)

◆ Remove the steaks from the pan and let them sit and reabsorb their juices.

◆ Keeping the skillet over high heat, add the shallot and cook until soft, about 3 to 5 minutes. Add the wine, and let it reduce (boil down) until it's thickened and syrupy. Toss in the parsley, and then take the skillet off the heat and add the remaining tablespoon of butter. Swirl the butter around until it's completely dissolved. Pour the red wine sauce over the steaks, and serve.

✳ My Favorite Hamburger

If you ask me, there are few things better than a good hamburger. My version of ground beef greatness is not for the staunch traditionalist. Dressed up and downright delicious, this is one of my favorite comfort meals—especially with crinkle-cut or seasoned curly fries. (Being lazy, I use the frozen ones, but when I'm a good go-girl, I opt for a side salad.)

TOTAL TIME: 20 minutes
ACTIVE TIME: 20 minutes
Serves 4

Get It
1⅓ pounds ground beef
1 teaspoon Worcestershire sauce
Salt and freshly ground black pepper
1 fresh sweet baguette (avoid the kind with lots of air pockets)
4 teaspoons unsalted butter, at room temperature
1 teaspoon vegetable oil

3 ounces thinly sliced cheddar cheese or crumbled blue cheese
2 tablespoons mayonnaise
½ clove garlic, peeled and pressed
20 spinach leaves
Ketchup

Go, Girl

◆ In a bowl mix the beef and Worcestershire sauce. Sprinkle generously with salt and add a grind or two of pepper. Shape the meat into oblong patties about 2 inches wide, 1 inch thick, and 6 inches long. Set them aside.

◆ Cut the baguette into four equal pieces. Slice each piece open and separate the halves. Spread ½ teaspoon butter on each of the eight halves, place them crust-side down on a baking sheet, and set it aside.

◆ In a large nonstick pan heat the oil over a moderately high flame and then reduce the heat to moderate.

◆ Cook the patties 3 to 4 minutes on each side for medium rare, longer for medium or well done. When you begin cooking the second side, add the cheese. If it doesn't melt to your liking, put the pan under the broiler for a minute (so long as it's oven-safe).

◆ While the burgers are cooking, put the baking sheet of baguettes under the broiler for 3 to 4 minutes, or until the tops are just golden but the bread is still soft.

◆ In a cup mix the mayonnaise and garlic. Spread it onto the bottom halves of the toasted baguettes, add a layer of spinach leaves, top with a hamburger patty, and finish with a hearty squirt of ketchup. Heaven.

✳ Slow-Cooked Beef Stew

I knew I adored chef, teacher, and award-winning cookbook author John Ash when our first encounter included spontaneously brainstorming about how to create a sensual foods kit. John's attitude to life—and cooking—is fun and approachable. When he sent me this recipe, he noted, "I'm a big fan of 'one-pot' meals. They're easy to make and they promote conviviality, since you dish them out right at the table." This pot of fun is based on an ancient Italian recipe called "Peposo," which is so named because it uses a lot of pepper. It's not last-minute enough to get it started twenty minutes before you've got guests at the table, but it is an almost effortless recipe that you begin in the morning, forget about all day (except for the delicious smell filling the house), and serve after sundown. Double it and you can feed nearly a dozen red-meat fans. John recommends you serve it with crusty bread topped with the braising liquid, along with mashed or roasted potatoes, polenta, or pasta. He also suggests you crack the pepper at the last moment, using a coffee grinder, a mortar and pestle, or the bottom of a heavy cast-iron pan rolled around on whole peppercorns.

TOTAL TIME: 8 to 10 hours
ACTIVE TIME: 20 minutes
Serves 4 to 6

Get It
For the stew:
2½ pounds lean stewing beef, cut into 2-inch squares
3 tablespoons olive oil

16 cloves garlic, peeled

2 tablespoons or so cracked black pepper (not ground)

4 cups canned diced tomatoes in juice

2 cups hearty red wine such as cabernet or zinfandel

1 cup chopped basil leaves

Salt

For the gremolata garnish:

3 large cloves garlic, peeled

1 cup packed parsley leaves

2 to 3 tablespoons finely grated lemon zest

½ teaspoon or so salt

Go, Girl

◆ Preheat the oven to 275°F.

◆ Brown the beef quickly in the olive oil in a large heavy pot, preferably ceramic or enamel. Pour off the fat and add all of the remaining stew ingredients, except the salt, to the pot.

◆ Cover the pot tightly, place it in the oven, and let the stew cook for 8 to 10 hours, until the meat is very tender. Alternatively you can let the stew simmer gently on the stove top over very low heat. Check the pot occasionally, and if the liquid begins to boil away, add a little boiling stock, wine, or water and lower the heat.

◆ Prepare the gremolata: Chop the garlic in a food processor. (If you don't have a food processor, chop the ingredients by hand.) Add the parsley and lemon, and pulse to finely chop it all. Be careful not to turn the mixture into a paste; it should be light and airy. Add salt to taste. Set the gremolata aside.

- Transfer the cooked meat to a deep platter and keep it warm. Degrease the cooking liquid if necessary by skimming the top and discarding any layer of grease. Add salt to taste. Return the meat to the braising liquid and serve the stew topped with a sprinkling of gremolata.

Get Out of the Kitchen!

Even armed with the fab recipes in this book, there comes a time when the party girl is too pressed or pooped for kitchen detail. That's the time to shirk stove-top responsibilities and shamelessly build your spread of ready-made items. There is nothing wrong with integrating store- or restaurant-bought food into your fete. In fact, there are times when cheap wooden chopsticks and Chinese boxes brimming with take-out treasures are the perfect thing. Even *Food & Wine* editor in chief Dana Cowin declares she's a fan of "anything that doesn't take time or money." She advises, "If there's a restaurant that makes something you love and your instinct says it's affordable, ask them if they can do something special for you that you can pick up and take home. They may not be able to completely cater for you, but they're likely to throw something together."

Want some ideas on how to make take-out magic? Consider the following purchased fare paired with homemade accents, and don't forget you can still add your own style by transferring your takeout to serving dishes or adding something homemade to your store-bought spread.

- **Chinese food:** You have a gazillion options—Peking duck, moo-shu pork, Mongolian beef. Add a few vegetable dishes and a side of rice, reheat them at home, serve them on pretty platters, and it's your very own ancient Chinese secret. Likewise Thai food.

- ◆ **Rotisserie chicken:** Lots of take-out places and supermarkets sell spectacular ready-made whole chickens. Local restaurants also may bag a bird for you, ideally with sides such as roasted veggies.

- ◆ **Pizza:** Try a new twist on an old standby. Call your favorite pizza parlor and ask if you can buy the pizza primped with toppings but not yet cooked. Ask for cooking instructions, pop it in the oven, and in an instant you're the chef. (Better yet, ask for just the disk-shaped dough and add your own toppings.)

- ◆ **Sushi:** It's expensive but an absolutely gorgeous appetizer or main course. Buy an array, set it out on something sexy with accompanying sides of soy sauce, pickled ginger, and wasabi, and don't forget the chopsticks.

✳

WHILE WRITING THIS book, I took a trip to New York and met a bunch of my foodie gal pals for dinner at party-girlfriend Kate Krader's apartment. Two *Food & Wine* editors, two *Martha Stewart Living* writers, a *Time Out New York* food critic, and I lolled on the floor and couches, sipping spiked sodas. We eventually passed around a Thai take-out menu and called in our order. When the food arrived, we ate on paper plates with plastic forks. With no kitchen duties, our host could spend all her time gossiping rather than prepping, and dinner was excellent.

8

Sidekicks

I AM NOT the type of girl who buys every kitchen gizmo and gadget. In fact, part of my recipe for a perfect party pad is to have a clean, minimalist environment, including my kitchen. As a result, I add new things to my cooking-equipment collection only when there's no way to work a recipe without them. Most of the time I create my own solutions. I've often rolled out pastry dough with a beer glass, baked cakes in a fish mold because it was the only deep-dish container I had (I later drew scales in icing), and used a pot in a pot instead of a double boiler. I'm currently addicted to "chicken under a cast-iron skillet," which would be "chicken under a brick" except I don't have a brick lying around. You don't need a professional kitchen in order to serve a great meal, nor do you need every single culinary contraption that hits the market. You just need to put on your problem-solving cap, enter the kitchen with an adventurous spirit, and learn as you go.

*

S ide dishes should be complements, not contenders, to your entrees. As lovers, not fighters, they bulk up your beef stew, soak up your seafood sauce, and add a special texture and flavor to your starring dish. Whenever you're in need of a sexy yet simple side ranging from starch to veggie, browse the options in this chapter, which are grouped by type and organized from easiest to most time-consuming.

Potatoes with Parsley

When you've got a main course with a savory sauce and you want to sex it up with a starch, this is one hot potato you won't want to pass up. It's easy to make, classic, and flexible enough to pair with everything from fish and chicken to red meat. If you're not serving them with something saucy, add more fresh herbs and additional seasonings, perk them up with butter and grated Parmesan cheese, or cook 'em crispy (read on for details). Otherwise, your 'taters will be pretty on the plate but a little Plain Jane in the mouth.

TOTAL TIME: 20 minutes
ACTIVE TIME: 5 minutes
Serves 4

Get It
8 new potatoes
Salt
1 tablespoon olive oil or butter

Freshly ground black pepper

1 tablespoon chopped fresh parsley

Go, Girl

◆ Peel the potatoes and cut them into bite-size wedges.

◆ Place the potatoes in a medium-size pot and pour in just enough water to cover them. Bring the water to a boil and add a generous pinch of salt. Turn down the heat to a simmer and let the potatoes cook until tender, about 5 minutes. (Test to make sure they're done—they should be firm, but a fork should be able to pierce them easily.)

◆ Immediately drain the potatoes. Let them sit for a minute to steam away excess moisture, and then toss them with the olive oil, more salt, pepper, and parsley. Serve immediately. FYI, if you prefer crispy edges, you can sauté the potatoes in a large sauté pan with a tablespoon of vegetable oil over medium heat before serving.

✳ Mashed Potatoes

There are a few things you must know to make outstanding mashed potatoes. First, don't overcook the potatoes, or the texture will suffer. Second, use a masher (affordable handheld gizmo). It's absolute torture to try to wing it with a fork (but worth it!). Finally, don't hold back on the dairy. It's the reason we all love mashed potatoes!

TOTAL TIME: 45 minutes

ACTIVE TIME: 15 minutes

Serves 4 to 6

Get It

2 pounds russet potatoes

½ onion, peeled and halved through the root

2 teaspoons salt

¼ pound (1 stick) softened butter, cut into chunks

¼ to ½ cup heavy cream

¼ teaspoon white pepper

Go, Girl

◆ Peel the potatoes, cut them into quarters, and drop them into a large pot of water. Add the onion and 1½ teaspoons of the salt.

◆ Bring the water to a boil and let the potatoes cook for about 15 minutes, or until you can easily pierce the center but they're not so tender that they fall apart.

◆ Immediately drain the potatoes and discard the onion. Return the potatoes to the empty pot.

◆ If there's water on the potatoes, stir them over medium heat until they dry. Remove the pot from the heat.

◆ Mash the potatoes with a masher. When they're creamy, beat in the butter.

◆ Heat the cream in a saucepan and then stir it into the potatoes a little at a time, using only as much as you need to get the consistency you want. Season with the remaining ½ teaspoon salt and the pepper. Taste again and add more salt if necessary.

◆ Keep your perfectly mashed potatoes warm in the pot and covered over low heat until you're ready to serve them, and go ahead and give yourself permission to scoop spoonfuls into your mouth. You won't be able to resist, so what's the point of trying?

Variations

Garlic Mashed Potatoes: Add a few cloves of roasted garlic (see Whole Roasted Garlic in Chapter 5).

Horseradish Mashed Potatoes: Add a few tablespoons of ready-made horseradish.

Potato Gratin

This dish embodies decadence without difficulty. An adaptation of a recipe made by chef and diehard Yankees fan Carmen Quagliata, whom I met while he was working at Napa Valley's Tra Vigne restaurant, it's pretty, creamy, and crunchy-crusted, and it can be made in individual ramekins or one big baking dish. Serve it anytime you're hankering for comfort food.

TOTAL TIME: 1 hour, 20 minutes
ACTIVE TIME: 20 minutes
Serves 4

Get It

4 large russet potatoes

1 tablespoon butter plus extra for coating the pan

2 teaspoons chopped garlic

1 pint heavy cream

Salt and freshly ground black pepper

¾ cup grated Parmesan cheese

2 teaspoons chopped thyme

Go, Girl

◆ Peel the potatoes and slice them as thin as possible, 1/8 inch or thinner.

◆ In a large saucepan melt the butter with the garlic, add the cream, season with salt and pepper, and bring to a simmer.

◆ Add the potatoes and remove the pan from the heat.

◆ Lightly butter an 8-inch square ceramic baking pan. Remove the potato slices from the cream, reserving the cream, and cover the bottom of the pan with a single layer of slightly overlapping potato slices. Sprinkle with some of the Parmesan and thyme. Repeat the process until the pan is three-fourths full. Pour the cream and garlic mixture over the potatoes.

◆ Cover the pan with foil and cook for 45 minutes in an oven preheated to 350°F; then remove the foil and let the top brown, about 10 more minutes.

◆ Remove the potatoes from the oven and let them rest for 15 minutes (so they hold together better) before serving.

Variations

Striped Gratin: Trade half the potatoes for layers of thinly sliced butternut squash or sweet potatoes.

Gratin with Greens: Add chopped Swiss chard leaves (greens only, not the stems) to the butter and garlic, and sauté.

Easy Cheesy Gratin: Add chunks of goat cheese, Brie, or any other cheese you have hanging around the house.

Horseradish Gratin: Grate 1/2 cup fresh horseradish, add it to the butter and garlic, and sprinkle it in with the potato layers.

 **Polenta**

Polenta is a fantastically savory and hearty cornmeal mush that's popular in Italy—and destined to become so in your kitchen. Sure, you can start from scratch and stir over a hot stove for at least half an hour, but why bother when you can buy huge tubes of prepared polenta? The ready-made roll starts as a rubbery chunk, but add a little heat, milk, and butter and you've got creamy cornmeal that's perfect as an appetizer or a side dish.

TOTAL TIME: 10 minutes
ACTIVE TIME: 10 minutes
Serves 4

Get It
1 18-ounce tube of ready-made polenta
1 cup milk
3 tablespoons unsalted butter
Salt

Go, Girl
◆ Chop the polenta into 1-inch chunks and throw them into a medium-size pot with the milk.
◆ Whisk the chunks over medium heat until they dissolve into a creamy mass. Add the butter, salt to taste, and keep the polenta warm in a covered pot until you're ready to serve. (Stir in more milk if it gets too thick.)

Variations

Mix in a ½ cup grated Parmesan cheese and a dollop of mascarpone
  cheese, and top with a few fresh sage leaves fried for a minute or two
  in butter—incredible appetizer.
Add a scoop of mushrooms sautéed in butter—another great starter.
Top with a hefty spoonful of fresh salsa—a lighter first course.
Top with a dollop of warmed tomato sauce—comfort-food classic.

Couscous

This fast-cooking side dish made from coarsely ground durum wheat is a
light, fluffy alternative to rice. Serve a basic style with any main course
that has a good deal of sauce, or go for a seasoned couscous when you
want to jazz up simple dishes like broiled seafood or chicken. Most stores
carry couscous with a variety of seasonings. All you need to do is buy a
box and boil water, and you're done.

TOTAL TIME: 20 minutes
ACTIVE TIME: 5 minutes
Serves 4

Get It

½ teaspoon salt
1 tablespoon olive oil or butter
1½ cups fast-cooking couscous

Go, Girl

- Follow the directions on the box, or, in a medium saucepan, boil 2 cups of water, the salt, and the olive oil.
- Stir in the couscous. Cover the pan, remove it from the heat, and let the couscous sit for 5 minutes.
- Fluff the stuff with a fork and serve.

Rice

This economically sound side dish is a party-girl staple. If you want white rice, which pairs well with dishes that need something to soak up their sauce, stick with basmati. For more formal affairs, go exotic with gorgeously dark and mysterious wild rice, which has a wonderfully nutty flavor and great texture.

TOTAL TIME: 20 minutes
ACTIVE TIME: 3 minutes
Serves 4

Get It
1 cup rice of choice
Salt

Go, Girl

- Follow the directions on the package. Rice preparation and the amount of water to use depend on what kind you buy.

◆ A surefire way to make perfect basmati (white rice) is to pour the rice into a medium pot and cover it with enough water so that when you touch the top of the rice with the tip of your thumb, the waterline comes up to the center of your knuckle. Add a dash of salt. Bring the water to a boil and immediately reduce the heat to simmer; cover the pot, let the rice steam for 20 minutes, and serve.

Orzo

This rice-shaped pasta is a sultry way to fill stomachs and plates without emptying your pocketbook. It's also ideal for the haphazard hostess who wants flare with her fillet of salmon or Sexy Mixed Seafood (see Chapter 7) but can't be bothered with doing much more than boiling water. This is a partner that's meant to complement more powerful main-course flavors, so don't serve this solo unless you add flavorful accompaniments such as reduced chicken broth, sautéed bacon, chopped onions, and peas.

TOTAL TIME: 20 minutes
ACTIVE TIME: 5 minutes
Serves 4

Get It
2 teaspoons salt
3 cups orzo
4 tablespoons unsalted butter, chopped into pieces
½ cup grated Parmesan cheese
1 teaspoon each of fresh herbs such as oregano, thyme, parsley, or chives

Go, Girl

◆ Bring a large pot of water to a boil, and add 1½ teaspoons of the salt. Stir in the orzo and boil for 8 to 10 minutes. Stir a few times along the way, and test to make sure the pasta does not overcook. (It should have a slight firmness.)

◆ Immediately drain the orzo in a colander, shaking to eliminate any excess water.

◆ Transfer the orzo to a serving bowl and add the butter, Parmesan, herbs, and remaining salt to taste.

✳ Haricots Verts

These fancy French green beans (say "ah-ree-ko-VEHR") are thin, delicate, and sometimes hard to find. (Go for gourmet grocers.) Thankfully, they're easy to prepare in any language. You can blanch them and stick them in salads, or serve them as entree sidekicks with a simple coat of sweet butter. Can't find the fancy beans? Go for the thinnest string beans you can find.

TOTAL TIME: 15 minutes
ACTIVE TIME: 5 minutes
Serves 4

Get It
Salt
½ pound haricots verts or slender green beans
1 tablespoon unsalted butter

Go, Girl

◆ Bring a large pot of water to a boil over high heat then add a generous sprinkle of salt.

◆ Wash and drain the beans, cut off and discard their tops, and toss the beans into the boiling water.

◆ Cook for 2 to 3 minutes, drain them immediately, toss them with the butter, and serve.

✳ Oven-Roasted Vegetable Skewers

Whenever you're stumped on what side dish to serve, stop here. Cooking veggies in a moderately hot oven results in rustic full flavors, and skewers bring a festive barbecue element to everyday roasted vegetables. Don't have skewers? Just throw the veggies into a lightly oiled pan instead. If you want sassier veggies, toss some balsamic vinegar and pressed garlic into your olive oil mix.

TOTAL TIME: 40 minutes
ACTIVE TIME: 10 minutes
Serves 4

Get It
¼ cup extra-virgin olive oil
½ teaspoon salt
Freshly ground black pepper
4 new potatoes, halved

8 broccoli florets

1 crookneck squash, sliced into ½-inch disks

1 zucchini, sliced into ½-inch disks

4 mushrooms, halved

4 small vine-ripened tomatoes, halved

Go, Girl

◆ Preheat the oven to 350°F.

◆ In a bowl mix the olive oil, salt, and pepper.

◆ Toss all of the vegetables in the oil, and slide a combination of each onto eight skewers.

◆ Roast the veggies on a baking sheet for 30 minutes, or until tender, and serve.

✳ Sautéed Asparagus

These sexy green spears go great with entrees. And the less you do to them, the better, since they're so darned good on their own. Asparagus is seasonal, so serve this dish often from early spring through the beginning of summer. FYI: Along with this stove-top recipe, you can also boil the spears until they're to your desired texture, strain, add a slab of butter, and serve.

TOTAL TIME: 20 minutes

ACTIVE TIME: 5 minutes

Serves 4 to 6

Get It

1½ pounds asparagus spears

1 tablespoon olive oil

2 large cloves garlic, minced (optional)

Salt and freshly ground black pepper

Go, Girl

◆ Slice off about an inch from the bottom ends of the spears. Discard the ends, and set the asparagus aside.

◆ Heat the olive oil in a large skillet over a medium flame. Add the garlic and sauté for 1 or 2 minutes; keep the heat low enough that the garlic does not begin to brown.

◆ Add the asparagus, just enough water to cover the bottom of the pan, and salt and pepper to taste. Cover the pan and let the asparagus steam for 10 minutes. Taste to see if it's as you like it—some people go for crunchier asparagus. If you like yours soft, it may need to cook longer.

◆ Cook the asparagus uncovered for a few final minutes, and serve.

✳ Sautéed Spinach with Garlic

Be strong to the finish with this gorgeous garlic-flavored spinach.

TOTAL TIME: 7 minutes

ACTIVE TIME: 7 minutes

Serves 4

Get It

4 teaspoons extra-virgin olive oil

2 cloves garlic, peeled and sliced thin

1 pound (about 16 loosely packed cups) baby spinach leaves

Salt

Go, Girl

◆ Heat the olive oil in a large skillet over a medium flame. Add the garlic and sauté for 1 or 2 minutes; keep the heat low enough that the garlic does not begin to brown.

◆ Add the spinach, turning it over frequently to help the leaves wilt evenly and contact the oil and garlic. When all the spinach is wilted, add a few sprinkles of salt, and serve.

✳

I RECENTLY MOVED to a place where I had a big enough patch of land to plant a vegetable garden. City girl that I am, after the first time I stuck lettuce seedlings, tiny tomato plants, and herbs into dirt, I jumped out of my bed each morning for about a month and suspiciously eyed the garden bed, honestly astounded that my plants were growing. Now when I need to add fresh flavor to a dish, I step outside and pluck my fill of chives, basil, sage, rosemary, and thyme. Sure, it saves time and money, but as goofy as it sounds, the best part is that it makes me proud because I grew it myself. You don't need to have access to the great outdoors to gain green-thumb momentum and harvest your own herbs. All you need is a sunny windowsill and attention to watering detail, and soon you can sprinkle tonight's potatoes with your own lovingly grown parsley.

9

Decadent Desserts

TWO RECURRING LAST-MINUTE scenarios play themselves out around my house. One is that friends drop by with little more than ten minutes' notice. The other is that I'm too busy writing, procrastinating, or lounging to prepare for entertaining. In either case it is not unusual for me to have to rummage through my cupboards to come up with instant food fabulousness. Sometimes I have all the ingredients I need to make a recipe. Other times I work with what I have, transforming portions of recipes I've learned into something new. Recently a group of friends pushed back from my dinner table, and I realized I hadn't thought about dessert. But two weeks before, I'd made Chocolate Toffee Crunch Cakes (see the recipe in this chapter), so I had straggler ingredients of caramels, chocolate chips, toffee, and cream. I also had half a pint of ice cream in the freezer. I slid into the kitchen, melted the caramels with a splash of cream, chopped the chips and toffee, and scooped the ice cream into bowls and slathered it with hot caramel, chocolate, and toffee. It was a scavenged sensation in ten minutes tops. The more I play in my kitchen, the easier it is to summon on-the-spot improvisation. You'll find the same is true for you.

*

Dessert is the course that puts your party-girl hospitality over the top. Like the appetizer, it's a superfluous touch that shows that you took your sweet and gracious sensibilities above and beyond the call of kitchen duty. Trust me: you can get party-girl props by whipping up sensational salads, outrageous entrees, and killer cocktails, but make dessert from scratch and you're suddenly a superstar. Hoist your haute-hostess status with the following recipes, which are organized from easiest to most time-consuming and guaranteed to glamorize your grand finale. Don't forget to offer coffee. It's a simple and very classy gesture.

*Strawberries and Sweet Cream

When you've got five minutes to fling dessert together, this is your savior. I serve it at all my picnics and luncheons, with the strawberries stacked high around the bowl of cream.

TOTAL TIME: 5 minutes
ACTIVE TIME: 5 minutes
Serves 4 to 6

Get It
1 cup sour cream (Don't go low-fat; it's not nearly as good.)
¼ to ½ cup brown sugar
1 large basket of strawberries (or more if you wish)

Go, Girl

◆ You can do this two ways. The first is to serve the sour cream in one bowl and the brown sugar in another and encourage guests to double dip. The second is to mix the sour cream and brown sugar until it's smooth, transfer it to a bowl in the center of a serving tray, and arrange the strawberries around the bowl.

◆ Supply a container in which guests can deposit the green tops.

Pineapple with Fiery Sugar Dip

During Thai cooking classes at The Oriental hotel in Bangkok, our instructor, "Chef San" (a.k.a. Sarnsern Gajaseni), rattled off the ingredients for this simple Thai temptation. It's a flavor explosion and an excellent example of how Southeast Asian cooking brings a party to the palate with a symphony of sour, salty, sweet, and hot. Seriously, you must try this at home.

TOTAL TIME: 10 minutes
ACTIVE TIME: 10 minutes
Serves 10 to 15

Get It

1 pineapple
1 cup sugar (ideally moist, fine-textured raw sugar, but white will do)
1½ teaspoons salt, or to taste
Fresh bird's-eye chili peppers, 1 minced and a few whole for garnish
    (available at Asian markets)

Go, Girl

◆ Cut off the pineapple skin, doing your darnedest not to take off too much of the tart-sweet insides. Slice the pineapple into 2- to 3-inch wedges and arrange them decoratively around a serving plate, leaving space in the center for the dip.

◆ Put the sugar in a mixing bowl and gradually add the salt, mixing thoroughly and tasting along the way, until the salt flavor comes through but does not overpower the sugar.

◆ With your hands, mash in the chili. (Be brave: no need for gloves if you don't put your finger in your eye—or someone else's—before you wash up.) You want to spread the chili flavor throughout the mix until it's got a seriously hot bite to it.

◆ Transfer the mix to a decorative bowl, garnish it with a whole chili or two, and place it in the center of the pineapple plate.

◆ Your friends won't know what to do with this when they first see it, so show them by dunking a pineapple chunk in the sugar dip. Once one guest takes the pineapple-dip plunge, it'll be the talk of the party.

Instant Banana Ice Cream

The next time you're about to throw away a browning banana, think again. Peel it, wrap it in plastic wrap, stick it in your freezer, and pull it out for this absurdly easy dessert. It's nothing short of magic.

TOTAL TIME: 5 minutes
ACTIVE TIME: 5 minutes
Serves 4

Get It

2 peeled and frozen bananas

⅓ cup toasted walnuts or pecans (optional; see Toasted Nuts in Chapter 5)

1 cup Homemade Caramel Sauce (optional; see the recipe in this chapter)

Go, Girl

◆ Cut the frozen bananas into bite-size pieces, put them in a blender, and blend on the lowest speed. The bananas will inevitably stick to the sides of the container, so turn off the blender, push them down to the blades, and blend again, repeating as necessary.

◆ Within seconds the banana mass will grow right before your eyes, whirling itself into a velvety cream.

◆ Immediately transfer the treat to serving bowls, top with the nuts and sauce, and try to convince your friends that it really is just banana.

✳ Almost Naughty Nectarine

When you're in the mood to serve something simply sophisticated and not too heavy, go for this dessert. It takes minutes to prepare; is delicate, sweet, and salty; and works even when you forget it in the oven for an extra half hour. The only bummer: it's seasonal along with the nectarines, which tend to be available spring through fall, with a peak season of mid-summer. Serve it with toasted nuts, a plate-side puddle of Homemade Caramel Sauce (see the recipe in this chapter), or on its own.

TOTAL TIME: 35 minutes

ACTIVE TIME: 5 minutes

Serves 4

Get It

1 tablespoon unsalted butter

1 tablespoon sugar

2 firm but ripe nectarines, halved and pitted

3 tablespoons Blue Castello cheese or other blue cheese

¼ cup toasted pecan halves for garnish (optional; see Toasted Nuts in
  Chapter 5 for toasting instructions)

Go, Girl

◆ Preheat the oven to 350°F.

◆ Melt the butter in a large saucepan over medium-high heat, stir in the
sugar, and place the nectarine halves flesh-side down in the pan.

◆ Cook for 2 minutes, or until the flesh is browned, scooting the fruit
around to coat them with as much sugar as possible.

◆ Put the nectarines flesh-side up in a baking dish, fill the centers with
equal portions of the cheese, and bake in the upper section of the oven

FROZEN GRAPES

Frozen grapes are nature's bite-size Popsicles. Just stick a bunch in the freezer,
pull them out after an hour, and serve immediately.

for 30 minutes, or until the cheese begins to brown and the fruit has softened.

◆ Serve warm on a small plate garnished with the nuts.

✳ Coffee Granita

Turn frozen coffee into an amped-up and fashionable finale with little more than a flick of the fork or food processor. Aside from the simplicity factor, the best thing about granita is that once you know how easy it is, you can confidently substitute any liquid flavor you want. Say "grah-nee-TAH" with an Italian accent or granité ("grah-nee-TAY") if you want to feel French.

TOTAL TIME: 1 hour
ACTIVE TIME: 10 minutes
Serves 4

Get It
2 cups warm espresso or strong coffee
¼ cup sugar
4 dollops of whipped cream (homemade or store-bought)
⅛ cup Grand Marnier (optional)

Go, Girl
◆ Mix the coffee and sugar until the sugar dissolves. Freeze the coffee in an ice cube tray.

◆ When it's completely frozen and you're ready to serve, get out the whipped cream and four martini glasses, or any clear serving bowls or glasses. Throw the frozen cubes into the food processor and, using the grater attachment, grate the coffee ice. (If you don't have a food processor, you can freeze the coffee in a thin layer on a baking pan and then scrape it with a fork.)

◆ Work fast here. Quickly transfer your granita to the glasses, top with whipped cream, drizzle Grand Marnier over the cream, and serve.

Variations

Mocha Granita: Add 2 tablespoons unsweetened cocoa powder to the coffee.

Irish Coffee Granita: Substitute a float of whiskey for the Grand Marnier.

Mexican Coffee Granita: Try a tequila topping.

Sleep-Friendly Coffee Granita: Use decaf.

✳ Homemade Caramel Sauce

This sauce is decadent, divinely simple, and a hot and creamy ticket to customizing any dessert with a dash of homemade heaven. Use it to drizzle over ice cream, decorate a dessert plate, or sugarcoat someone you love. Feeling frisky? Flavor the cream with coffee or chocolate for unusual caramel combos. Also see Chocolate Toffee Crunch Cakes (in this chapter) for a way to make caramel sauce with store-bought candy and cream.

TOTAL TIME: 10 minutes
ACTIVE TIME: 5 minutes
Makes 2½ cups

Get It

2 cups brown sugar

4 tablespoons (½ stick) unsalted butter

1½ cups cream

1 teaspoon vanilla extract

Go, Girl

◆ Bring all the ingredients to a boil in a heavy pot, stirring occasionally. Let the sauce simmer for a few minutes, cool until it's just warm, and serve.

*Puff Daddies, a.k.a. Fast Fruit Tarts

L.A.-based caterer-to-the-stars Phillip Weingarten taught me this elegant last-minute dessert. It takes no time or talent and is glamorous enough for the most special occasions. He calls it a *galette* (French for a flat, pastry-dough-based cake or tart). I call it brilliant. Don't forget to defrost the pastry dough a half hour before you're ready to bake.

TOTAL TIME: 30 minutes
ACTIVE TIME: 10 minutes
Serves 6

Get It

⅔ cup unsalted butter plus 1 teaspoon for greasing the pan

1 10″ × 14″ sheet ready-made pastry dough, defrosted (Pepperidge Farm makes a good one.)

3 cups blueberries or peeled and very thinly sliced pear or apple wedges

¾ cup sugar

6 scoops vanilla ice cream (optional)

1 cup Homemade Caramel Sauce (optional; see the preceding recipe)

Go, Girl

◆ Preheat the oven to 375°F.

◆ Melt the ⅔ cup butter in a saucepan over low heat. Set it aside.

◆ Grease a baking sheet with the remaining 1 teaspoon butter.

◆ On a floured surface, unroll the dough, cut it into six equal squares, and transfer the squares to the baking sheet.

◆ Cover each square with ½ cup of the berries or with enough pear or apple slices, attractively overlapping, to blanket all but the pastry edges.

◆ Using a basting brush or a spoon, paint the fruit with the melted butter, and then sprinkle each square with 2 tablespoons of the sugar.

◆ Pop them into the oven and bake for 20 minutes, or until the pastry is golden and the fruit is tender.

◆ Serve with ice cream and a decorative drizzle of caramel sauce, and your guests will think you graduated from the Culinary Academy.

✳ Sweet Bananas and Salty Coconut

Party girls get big bonus points for turning guests on to something new. This wild Thai dessert definitely falls into that category. Sweet and salty, creamy and light, it's an adaptation from a recipe I was taught by chef Tamanoon Punchun at Mom Tri's Boathouse, a resort and cooking school on Thailand's island of Phuket. It may seem weird, but don't skip this one. It's too good. Also, use colored plates. White on white went out of fashion with "Miami Vice."

TOTAL TIME: 20 minutes
ACTIVE TIME: 5 minutes
Serves 4

Get It
4 cups sugar
8 small near-ripe bananas or 4 large just-ripe bananas
1 cup canned coconut milk
Salt
4 scoops vanilla ice cream or Instant Banana Ice Cream (see the recipe
　　earlier in this chapter; optional)
¼ cup toasted peanuts (optional; see Toasted Nuts in Chapter 5)
4 sprigs of fresh mint (optional)

Go, Girl
◆ In a pot bring 2 cups of water and the sugar to a boil.
◆ Add the bananas and let them simmer for 15 to 20 minutes, or until they've absorbed some syrup but are still firm enough to hold their form. Remove the bananas and set them aside. Discard the syrup.
◆ In a separate pot heat the coconut milk to a simmer and let it reduce to a creamlike consistency (by simmering and thus losing some of its moisture through evaporation). Season it with enough salt so that it is pleasantly but not overly salty.

◆ Pour the heated coconut milk into four rimmed and colorful dessert plates or shallow bowls. Top each with one large or two small bananas, and serve with or without ice cream, peanuts, and mint sprigs.

Strawberry and Rhubarb Cobbler

Fresh out of college my roommate Sarah Klein and I teamed up on lots of last-minute dinner parties. This affordable, easy, and bright red sweet-and-sour sensation was her dessert standby, and today it's still one of mine. Make it yours too, served à la mode or on its own.

TOTAL TIME: 40 minutes
ACTIVE TIME: 20 minutes
Serves 6

Get It
¼ pound (1 stick) softened unsalted butter plus 1 teaspoon for greasing
    the pan
¾ cup all-purpose flour
¾ cup sugar
¾ cup rolled oats
¼ teaspoon ground cardamom
½ teaspoon cinnamon
Generous pinch of salt
4 stalks rhubarb, cut into ½-inch chunks (about 3 cups)
1 pound strawberries, washed, hulled, and sliced (about 4 cups)

Go, Girl

◆ Preheat the oven to 375°F. Grease a 9-inch baking dish with the 1 teaspoon butter.

◆ For the topping, mix the flour, ½ cup of the sugar, oats, cardamom, cinnamon, salt, and the ¼ pound butter together with your fingers and set aside.

◆ Mix the rhubarb and strawberries together with the remaining ¼ cup sugar. Pour the fruit into the baking dish.

◆ Press the crumbled topping into large chunks and then break it into smaller chunks over the fruit to cover.

◆ Bake the cobbler for 40 minutes, or until the filling bubbles and the topping slightly browns.

◆ Serve warm or at room temperature.

Chocolate-Dipped Desires

Dip anything in chocolate and it's instantly seductive. Get creative: Scour the pantry for chocolate-compatible possibilities. Think strawberries, raspberries, banana slices, dried fruits such as mango spears or apricots, dates, pretzel sticks, frozen peanut-butter balls, fingers, and toes. This is one instance where double dipping is not only acceptable but also perhaps preferable. After your dippers emerge from the chocolate, consider rolling them in colored sprinkles, crushed toasted nuts, or cocoa powder, all of which not only add flare but also hide any visual imperfections. (Chocolate is fickle when melted and can "bloom," or develop a dull, whitish sheen, when subjected to too high or low temperatures. It still tastes good but won't look as pretty. Rolling your dipped treats in cocoa powder is a decorative disguise.) For a real flavor kick, add a sprinkle or two of rock salt, which perks up the chocolate flavor on your palate.

TOTAL TIME: 15 minutes
ACTIVE TIME: 15 minutes
Serves 4

Get It

4 ounces good-quality baking chocolate (like Scharffen Berger
    semisweet), chopped
Things to dip
Pinch of rock or kosher salt (optional)
¼ cup unsweetened cocoa powder

Go, Girl

◆ Melt the chocolate in a double boiler (or a small pot inside a larger pot one-quarter filled with water) of barely simmering water. You can also use the microwave set on medium (50 percent) power.
◆ Let the chocolate cool to lukewarm. Dip your treats into the chocolate, sprinkle with salt, roll in cocoa powder, and then let them chill in the fridge.
◆ Serve on a dramatic tray, cutting board, or checkerboard.

✳ Half-Homemade Sundaes

Build-your-own desserts take the pressure off the party girl and delight the sticky-faced kid in every guest. Set up the toppings in advance in individual serving bowls, pull the ice cream out of the freezer, and it's show time.

TOTAL TIME: 20 minutes

ACTIVE TIME: 20 minutes

Serves 4

Get It

1 pint vanilla ice cream

1 cup warm Homemade Caramel Sauce (earlier in this chapter)

½ cup toasted pecans, walnuts, or almonds, chopped (optional; see Toasted Nuts in Chapter 5)

2 ounces good-quality semisweet baking chocolate, shaved with a vegetable peeler (optional)

4 cherries (optional)

Fresh whipped cream (optional)

Go, Girl

◆ Distribute the ice cream into four bowls, and serve with your selection of toppings.

✳ Double-Chocolate Biscotti

. . . .

An awesome arm ornament for ice cream or coffee, these crunchy twice-baked Italian biscuits are also the ultimate filling for the chocolate lover's cookie jar.

TOTAL TIME: 45 minutes
ACTIVE TIME: 15 minutes
Makes about 16

Get It

8 tablespoons (1 stick) softened unsalted butter plus 1 teaspoon for
    greasing the pan

⅔ cup sugar

2 eggs

1 teaspoon salt

1 teaspoon baking powder

⅔ cup unsweetened cocoa powder (I like Scharffen Berger; see the
    Resource Guide for details.)

1½ cups all-purpose flour

½ cup semisweet chocolate chips (See's brand rocks! See the Resource
    Guide for details.)

½ cup toasted almond slivers (optional; for toasting tips see Toasted Nuts
    in Chapter 5)

Go, Girl

◆ Preheat the oven to 350°F. Grease a baking sheet with the 1 teaspoon
butter.

◆ In a mixing bowl beat the 8 tablespoons butter and the sugar. Add the
eggs and mix well. Add the salt, baking powder, cocoa, and flour, and mix
again. Toss in the chocolate chips and almonds and combine well.

◆ With wetted hands, scoop the dough out of the bowl and shape it on
the baking sheet into a long, flat log about 1 inch high and 5 inches wide.

- Bake the log for 15 minutes. Leaving the oven on, remove the log and let it cool slightly; then slice it with a serrated knife into 1-inch-thick biscuits.
- Lay the biscuits out on the baking sheet and return it to the oven for another 15 minutes, or until the biscotti are slightly toasted (just firm to the touch).
- Cool, stack, and serve.

✳Chocolate Crepes

Delicate, light, and easily prepared ahead of time, these "KRAYPS," or exquisite paper-thin egg-based pancakes, elegantly coddle anything from chocolate and ice cream to fresh fruit and cream. For other filling options, see the end of the recipe.

TOTAL TIME: 1 hour, 15 minutes
ACTIVE TIME: 20 minutes
Makes 4

Get It
2 eggs
Dash of sugar
1½ teaspoons water
4 teaspoons all-purpose flour
1½ teaspoons milk
1 tablespoon butter (approximate, for coating the pan)

5 ounces good-quality semisweet chocolate
Powdered sugar for garnish

Go, Girl

◆ Combine the eggs, sugar, and water in a mixing bowl, and beat well. Whip in the flour and milk. Let the batter chill in the fridge for an hour.

◆ Heat a 6-inch nonstick pan (or larger if you don't have a small one), and add enough butter to just coat the bottom. Drop in a tablespoon or two of the batter, and tilt the pan to spread it evenly over the bottom into a paper-thin pancake.

◆ Cook the crepe for about 1 minute, or until it's golden brown on the bottom. Flip the crepe and cook for another 30 seconds.

◆ Remove the crepe with a spatula and set it on a plate. Repeat the process with the remaining batter, regreasing the pan for each crepe. (You're likely to get better with practice, but you should have enough batter to ruin a few trial runs.) Set the crepes aside.

◆ Just before you're ready to serve, melt the chocolate in a double boiler (or a small pot inside a larger pot one-quarter filled with water) of barely simmering water. Try not to eat it before it gets to the crepe.

◆ Lay a crepe flat on a dessert plate, spread ¼ of the chocolate in the center of the crepe, and fold the edges inward as though you're wrapping a gift (which, in a sense, you are). Flip it over so the edges are underneath, and sprinkle powdered sugar over the top. Repeat for all your crepes, put on French bistro music, and sip Grand Marnier from a snifter.

Variations

Fill your dessert crepes with any of the following devilishly tasty options.

Sweetened berries: In a pot combine 2 cups blueberries or strawberries, ½ cup sugar, and 2 tablespoons water, and cook over medium heat until the berries are soft and settled in a purple syrup, about 10 minutes. Cool slightly before filling the crepe.

Instant Banana Ice Cream or store-bought ice cream and Homemade Caramel Sauce (see both recipes earlier in this chapter).

Chocolate Toffee Crunch Cakes

These may be the sexiest chocolate cakes you'll ever taste, and the easiest ones you'll ever make. If that's not enough to inspire you to put on your apron, consider that they're individual, which means everyone gets his or her own fancy dessert at your next fete. Perky, pretty, and very talented pastry chef Marika Shimamoto Doob from San Francisco's Hawthorne Lane turned me on to this incredibly moist and chocolaty recipe, which she simplified so home chefs can have a fling with four-star flavor.

TOTAL TIME: 50 minutes
ACTIVE TIME: 35 minutes
Serves 6

Get It
For the cakes:
¼ cup milk
2 tablespoons heavy cream

⅓ cup semisweet chocolate chips

2 tablespoons unsweetened cocoa powder

4 tablespoons (½ stick) unsalted butter

⅓ cup sugar

⅓ cup plus 1 tablespoon all-purpose flour

¼ teaspoon baking soda

⅛ teaspoon baking powder

Pinch of salt

1 egg

½ teaspoon vanilla extract

¼ cup toffee, chopped into small pieces

Vanilla ice cream (optional)

For the caramel topping:

5 pieces chewy caramel

1½ tablespoons cream

For the chocolate sauce:

½ cup semisweet chocolate chips

1 tablespoon unsalted butter

¼ cup heavy cream

Go, Girl

◆ Prepare the cakes: Preheat the oven to 275°F. Moderately coat six cups of a nonstick standard-size muffin pan with vegetable spray (or butter). Cut six rounds of parchment paper to fit the bottoms (or you can use paper cup liners) and insert them in the cups.

◆ Fill a medium-size pot halfway with water and bring it to a boil. Reduce the heat so the water is steaming but not simmering. In a heat-proof bowl (large enough to fit over the pot) combine the milk, cream, chocolate chips, cocoa powder, butter, and sugar. Place the bowl over the steaming water. Heat for a few minutes, stirring frequently, until the chocolate is melted and the mixture is smooth. Remove the bowl from the heat.

◆ Sift the flour, baking soda, baking powder, and salt together. Add the sifted ingredients to the chocolate liquid in the bowl, and mix until the batter is smooth. Whisk in the egg and vanilla.

◆ Fill the six molds a little more than halfway with batter. Bake for 12 minutes, rotate the pan, and then bake another 8 minutes. Remove the tin from the oven and let the cakes cool for 5 to 10 minutes.

◆ While the cakes are baking, prepare the caramel topping: In a very small pot combine the caramels and cream. Cook over low heat, stirring frequently, until the caramels are melted and the mixture is smooth. Remove the pot from the heat and keep it at room temperature. Before use, if the caramel is too hard, gently heat it until just warm to the touch.

◆ Prepare the chocolate sauce: Fill a medium-size pot halfway with water and bring it to a boil. Reduce the heat so the water is steaming but not simmering. Combine the chocolate chips, butter, and cream in a heat-proof bowl and place it over the steaming water. Heat, stirring occasion-ally, until the chocolate is melted and the mixture is smooth. Keep it at room temperature, or refrigerate it and reheat it when you're ready to serve.

◆ Assemble the cakes: Run a knife around each cooled cake, gently lift it out of the muffin tin, and peel off the parchment paper. Place one cake in the middle of each plate and drizzle caramel and chocolate sauce over each cake. Top with chopped toffee and serve with vanilla ice cream.

DECADENT DESIGNS

One of the best ways to chocolate-coat Chocolate Toffee Crunch Cakes or manage the design of all your dressings is to invest in a plastic squeeze bottle. As a cheap champ for decoratively drizzling sauces, it can squirt squiggly lines of chocolate or caramel onto your dessert and get graphic with sauces for entrees and sides.

Other ways to add decorative oomph to plated desserts: First, you can pour powdered sugar into a small sifter or a fine sieve and dust it over the whole thing. If white doesn't work with your color combo, go for cocoa powder, or take a vegetable peeler to bittersweet chocolate and shave curls over your dessert. Remember that color contrast is good here. Add a sprig of mint or lavender, a fresh flower, a few berries, or a sliced strawberry fanned like a hand of cards, and you're golden. A more Martha Stewart–like alternative is a stencil: Cut out a paper heart, star, or whatever you want, place it directly on the dessert, and sift away. When you remove the paper (carefully), the shape will be outlined by the sugar or cocoa. Conversely, if you want a powder-filled shape on a powderless backdrop, cut the shape out of the center of a piece of paper big enough to cover the dessert, leaving the rest of the paper intact (or taping your incision that made its way to the middle). Place the paper stencil over the dessert and sift the powder over the cutout area. Voilà!

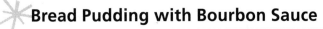

Bread Pudding with Bourbon Sauce

While waitressing my way through college in Berkeley, I worked at a Cajun-inspired restaurant called The Oxford Cafe. It's long gone now, and all that remains are my nightmares about the time I dashed into the court-yard and unintentionally stepped on a bird's head, and my dreams of the outrageously rich bread pudding, which I've done my best to re-create here. It's utterly over the top and perfect for midwinter love affairs with food, friends, or anyone whose heart and stomach you want to fill.

TOTAL TIME: 3 hours

ACTIVE TIME: 20 minutes

Serves 6

Get It

3 eggs

2 cups milk

1¼ cups sugar plus ¼ cup for the sauce

2 teaspoons vanilla extract

Dash of cinnamon

¾ of a sweet baguette, at least 1 or 2 days old, cut into 1-inch pieces, torn in half

¼ cup golden raisins, currants, or regular raisins, or a mix

½ cup (1 stick) unsalted butter

½ cup bourbon (I like lots of bourbon. Use less if you don't.)

Go, Girl

◆ In a large bowl mix the eggs, milk, 1¼ cups sugar, vanilla, and cinnamon. Pour the mixture into an 8-inch baking dish. Add the bread, submerging the pieces as much as possible, and the raisins. Cover and refrigerate for at least 1½ hours, or until the bread is very soggy.

◆ Preheat the oven to 350°F and cook for 1½ hours, or until the top is crunchy and golden. After removing the pudding from the oven, allow it to sit for 20 minutes.

◆ While the pudding is baking, make the sauce: Melt the butter in a small pot over medium heat. Stir in the remaining ¼ cup sugar and the bourbon, and heat for about 5 minutes. Keep it warm over low heat until you're ready to serve.

◆ Cut the bread pudding into thick squares, transfer them to plates, and ladle ¼ cup bourbon sauce over each.

◆ Serve, call a designated driver, and prepare for marriage proposals.

✳ Flan

Spain's answer to France's crème caramel is creamy, deceivingly simple, and beautiful with its dark brown caramel coating. It's also perfect for large formal parties provided you have enough ramekins to go around. (If you don't, you can always make one big flan in an ovenproof baking dish and serve it family style.) Tip: This is one of those recipes where it's good to carefully read it all the way through before you begin.

TOTAL TIME: 1 hour, 30 minutes
ACTIVE TIME: 30 minutes
Serves 6

Get It

1½ cups sugar

¼ cup water

4 eggs

Dash of salt

2 cups cream or milk

Go, Girl

◆ Combine 1 cup of the sugar and the water in a heavy saucepan. Cook the mixture over medium heat, stirring occasionally, until it's golden brown, about 20 minutes.

◆ Pour equal amounts of the caramelized sugar into six 4-ounce oven-proof ramekins and set them aside.

◆ Preheat the oven to 325°F.

◆ Separate two of the eggs and discard the whites. Place the two yolks and the two whole eggs in a mixing bowl, add the remaining ½ cup sugar and the salt, and beat until smooth.

◆ Heat the cream in a saucepan until it's steaming, and then add it to the egg mixture in a steady stream, stirring constantly.

◆ Pour the cream mixture over the caramel-lined ramekins.

◆ Place the ramekins in a deep baking pan. Pour enough hot water into the pan so that the ramekins are two-thirds submerged, with the tops about 1 inch higher than the water level.

◆ Cover the pan with aluminum foil and bake for approximately 30 minutes, or until the flans are set but still jiggling when moved.

◆ Let the flans cool, and then chill them in the fridge. When you're ready to serve, run a knife around the edge of each cup, invert the flan directly onto a dessert plate, and give it a little smack on its bottom.

(I know what you're thinking and I'm not going to say it.) You're ready for flan fare.

✳ The Cheese Course

If you don't want to end the meal on an overtly sweet note, serve a few very special cheeses. Powwow with a cheese purveyor to select two or three wedges. Divide the cheese into single servings (each about the size of a walnut in the shell), and arrange them on individual dessert plates with a few slices of bread, a pretty pile of toasted nuts, a teaspoon of honey, and a petite serving of fruit such as grapes, figs, or sliced pears or apples. For cheese details see Chapter 4.

✳

I LEARNED AN ornamental trick while dining at San Francisco's chichi Campton Place, which served the most beautiful frosted black Corinth grapes ("champagne grapes," or tiny berries better known as currants when dried) with a petite plate of after-dinner treats. The grapes glistened as though they'd just seen snow and tasted like they'd been kissed by fairy dust. I asked the waiter how it was done, and he clued me in to this slick sugarcoating trick that glamorizes all it graces. For fun and sweet flavor, spray a water mist onto minigrapes, mint leaves, or small flowers, and then sprinkle them generously with superfine sugar (available in the baking section at most upscale grocers). Let them dry, and then add them to your cheese or dessert plates.

10

Liquid Pleasures

UPON RETURNING FROM four days of cooking classes in Thailand, I threw a Thai-themed patio party complete with hot-as-hell curry, white rice, and Pineapple with Fiery Sugar Dip (Chapter 9). At the last minute I realized I also needed a cocktail that could meet the needs of the masses and stick with my Southeast Asian scene. I grabbed some leftover tamarind paste—which, I'd just learned, is an exotic sweet-and-sour sauce—added it to a pitcher of margaritas, and stuck four-inch lemongrass pieces into a cup for self-service swizzle sticks, and the instantly legendary Thai Margarita was born. I can't say that it was all that different from my regular margaritas, which also happen to be pretty damn good, but the secret to great entertaining is often about putting a new spin on old tricks. Next time you're playing bartender, scout your kitchen to see how you can customize your drinks in both flavor and fashion.

Take note, party girls. Drinks are the anchors of any event. After you greet your party-goers and hang coats and purses, you should barely bat a mascara-coated lash before offering your guests a beverage. Once they have a glass in hand, they're part of the party, armed with something to sip and a passport to mingle.

Unless you have the time and cash to stock and manage a full bar (yeah, right), the classiest way to get off the drink-service hook is to offer one fantastic specialty cocktail. Make it especially creative (not too sweet, sour, or blatantly strong) and serve it with style, and it'll be the libation life of the party—even when you are also serving wine and beer. The one-drink wonder is a particularly good tactic if you're hosting a lot of people, because keeping the glasses full of good wine and beer can be costly—plus you can (and should) make a big batch and keep the drinks flowing without working too hard. If you go with this supreme theme, don't forget to offer nonalcoholic choices. As a minimum requirement, have sparkling water and sodas on hand. If you're splurging, offer an array of designer pops and flavored waters. Also, for more formal affairs serve coffee, always, at the end of every dinner party, with milk and sugar on the side.

A savvy hostess knows that when it comes to cocktails, image is everything, so dress up your drinks. Slice limes paper-thin and float 'em atop your margaritas. Pick up playful swizzle sticks and plunk them in cocktails served in rocks glasses. Shade your sangria with paper umbrellas. Hang a plastic monkey from your martini. The point for every last detail of the party-girl party is to make it fun, so use your imagination.

A word on glassware: If your guests lose track of their wine goblets or cocktail glasses, it's the sign of a good party. An indication of a great party is a hostess who troubleshoots the ditched-dirty-glass scenario by labeling the glasses. Use fun stickers from your favorite cartoon characters, affix a small name tag, or have guests decorate their own ID labels (with art supplies provided by you, of course). Whatever you do, this simple trick will free you up from washing glasses mid-fiesta.

Even more important than how your drinks look is that you have enough. Only you know how thirsty your friends are. If everyone's drinking in moderation (Ha!) five bottles of wine will do for a dinner party of ten. Throwing a beer bash? No doubt ten pals can put away at least five six-packs. Springing for cocktails? You should be able to spike sixteen drinks with a 750 ml bottle of booze. Do the math and buy accordingly.

One more way to keep the drink department in order: Set up an inviting self-service bar area and leave the legwork to your guests. Create a cocktail station with all the necessities, and when you're busy, bar business can continue without you. Make refills easily accessible and self-serve or you'll break your stylish stride trying to keep the fun flowing. Any seasoned hostess will tell you there's nothing worse than an empty glass.

Now peruse the decadent drink recipes herewith and determine what works with your party plan. Not your everyday rum-and-Cokes, these luscious liquids—arranged from the most innocent inventions to the most potent and complex concoctions—take a small amount of effort and make a big impression. Pick your potion, toast your friends, and bottoms up.

✳ Fancy Water

This is one of my favorite tricks because it is effortless and has seemingly sophisticated results. You can turn tap water into a liquid luxury in less than five minutes with this recipe, which infuses any beverage with refreshing, clean, and subtle flavor.

Get It
Water
1 cucumber*

Get creative: substitute anything you like, such as a halved lemon or orange, sliced radishes, lemon grass, or crushed mint.

Go, Girl
- About 2 to 6 hours before guests arrive, fill a pitcher with water.
- Peel the whole cucumber, place it in the water, and chill.
- Remove the cuke and serve.

✳ Shirley Temple

Let your designated drivers live a little. This pink cheap-thrills nonalcoholic drink looks and tastes just as good as it did when you were living it up at a fancy restaurant with your parents. Only, this time you can have as many cherries as you want. Want to get wicked? Add a shot of vodka and—voilà!—it's a Squirrelly Temple.

Get It
Ice
1 splash grenadine

8 ounces 7-Up, or more if necessary

2 to 3 maraschino cherries

Go, Girl

- ◆ Fill a tall glass with ice, add a healthy dash of grenadine, and top with 7-Up.
- ◆ Add a cherry or two and relive your youth.

# Mexican Hot Chocolate

Since this warm and frothy favorite is guaranteed to warm the hearts and tummies of any chocolate-milk lover, the makings for it should be on hand at all times. Throw it together in less than five minutes and impress your guests with its unique flavor kissed with cinnamon and a hint of nuttiness from ground cocoa nibs (roasted shelled cocoa beans).

Get It

1 cup milk

2 solid chocolate sections of Ibarra Mexican hot chocolate (available at most grocery stores with ethnic foods)

Go, Girl

- ◆ In a pot combine the milk and chocolate.
- ◆ Cook over medium heat, whisking occasionally, until the chocolate has melted and the milk is frothy, and pour the lusty liquid into mugs.

◆ If you can resist eating the chocolate dregs at the bottom of the pot, stir them into the mugs. Otherwise, devour when no one's looking.

Variation
Add a shot of tequila and call it Mexican Hot Shot Chocolate.

Watermelon Aqua Fresca

Award-winning chef and cookbook author John Ash loves watermelon drinks. He anted up this sweetly sober aqua fresca recipe, which is a refreshing and red variation of the fresh-fruit drinks popular in Mexico and Latin America.

Serves 2 to 4

Get It
4 cups watermelon, rind removed, and coarsely chopped
Juice of 1 medium fresh lime
1 cup crushed ice
1 tablespoon superfine sugar (available in the baking section of most
   upscale grocers)
Mint sprigs
Orange wheels

Go, Girl
◆ Put the watermelon and lime juice in a blender or food processor and pulse briefly a few times to break down the flesh but keep the seeds whole.

- ◆ Strain the mixture through a fine strainer, and discard the seeds.
- ◆ Return the juice to the blender, add the ice and sugar to taste, and blend until smooth. Pour the mixture into tall glasses, and garnish with mint sprigs and orange wheels.

✳ Budget-Minded Bubbly

A great way to get away with serving absurdly inexpensive sparkling wine is to mix it with something else. In fact, even champagne snobs know not to pull out the pricey bubbly when it's a mimosa (sparkling wine and orange juice) in the making. Next time you're popping the cork for breakfast, brunch, lunch, dinner, cocktails, or a double bubble bath, consider

---

POP YOUR TOP

Sure, you can dramatically blast your cork across the room when opening sparkling wine, but I prefer the subtler and more sophisticated approach, which also stops the bubbly from overflowing onto the floor. To open your bottle, remove the foil covering the cork, hold the bottle at a 45-degree angle, remove the wire hood while holding down the cork in case it wants to make an early exit, cover the cork with a cloth napkin, and while holding the cork through the napkin, slowly turn the *bottle* (not the cork). The cork should disengage quietly (sorry, no big pop here), and if your bottle's still at a 45-degree angle, no bubbly will make a break for it until you begin to pour.

---

creating fizzy and affordable fun by adding any of the following mixers to your glass of sparkling wine.

Get It

1 bottle of sparkling wine
Mixer of choice (see the following list)

Go, Girl

◆ Pour the bubbly.
◆ Add a splash of orange juice to make a mimosa.
◆ Add a hefty splash of nectar de pêche (peach nectar; I like Williams-Sonoma's $8 variety, but any nectar will do), and you're serving Bellinis.
◆ Add crème de cassis and you're going beautifully burgundy with a Kir Royale.
◆ Or add any fruit juice you like and call it your own concoction.

Bianco Sour

Festive, slightly fizzy, light, and citrusy, this refreshing drink is ideal for daytime because it's got just enough booze to give you a buzz, but not so much that you go down with the sun. Tip: Multiply the recipe by ten and serve it in a pitcher.

Get It

3 ounces Martini and Rossi Bianco (a sweet vermouth available at most liquor stores)
3 ounces ginger ale

¼ lemon

Crushed ice

Go, Girl

♦ In a glass combine the Bianco and ginger ale. Squeeze the lemon into the glass, and then toss it in. Fill the glass with ice. Betcha can't drink just one.

✳ Sangria

Whether your fiesta is big, budget, or big-budget, this red wine punch is the perfect way to get a lot of people feeling happy without blowing excess cash. Besides, floating fruit is fun.

Makes 8 glasses of potent punch

Get It

1 cup sugar

1 cinnamon stick

1 lemon, sliced thin

1 orange, sliced thin

1 750 ml bottle red wine

1 750 ml bottle white wine

2 ounces brandy

Sliced strawberries, pineapple, peaches, nectarines, or any other fruit you want to see float (optional)

Ice

Go, Girl

◆ In a pitcher mix the sugar, cinnamon stick, lemon, orange, wines, and brandy. Refrigerate the mix for as long as you can stand it—ideally over-night, but at least 3 hours.

◆ Toss in the additional fruit just before serving, then fill each glass with ice and sangria. Olé!

Lovely Lillet

Originating in Bordeaux, France, this sexy-smooth blend of wine and fruit liqueurs is elegant and effortless. Pronounced "li-LAY," it's available at most liquor stores, extremely affordable, and a refined way to kick off any

---

SAKE

So sexy and smooth, so easy going down, and way fun when served in those cute Japanese cups (although martini glasses with a cucumber-wheel garnish are pretty darned festive, too), rice wine is a sultry alternative to wine made from grapes, especially when you're serving silky things like oysters, creamy dishes, or straightforward meats or fish. Go for one of the premium chilled varieties—no muss, no heating fuss, and far more sophisticated than the everyday hot stuff. Don't forget to garnish with a cucumber wheel, which you can make extra-fancy if you adapt the guidelines in "Whimsical Lemon Wheels" (in this chapter).

luncheon or dinner. Beware: The bottle empties faster than you can say *Merci beaucoup.*

Get It

White lillet, enough to fill a glass
Ice
1 orange wheel or wedge

Go, Girl

◆ Pour the lillet over ice in a rocks glass and serve with the orange wheel for garnish. *Très magnifique!*

Purple Haze

It's not as psychedelic as the days of Jimi Hendrix, but this hot, semisweet purple party-starter can put things into a colorful perspective. Buy cheap sake and put the savings toward pricey Chambord (around twenty bucks, last I looked). The raspberry liqueur's an investment, but on the bright side, its round bottle looks great on the bar.

Get It

10 ounces sake
1 ounce Chambord (black raspberry liqueur)

Go, Girl

◆ Heat the sake, pour it into a glass, and add the Chambord.
◆ Now move over, Rover, and let Jimi take over.

Bourbon Highball

It's Grandpa's drink for sure, but this sophisticate is a prime example of why with age comes wisdom. Not too sweet, nor too harsh, this thirst quencher takes the velvet-glove approach with sucker-punch effects.

Get It
Ice

2 ounces bourbon (the higher the quality, the better)

6 ounces ginger ale or soda water

1 lemon wedge

Go, Girl
◆ Fill a highball glass (a tall, skinny glass; or any glass, for that matter) with ice, and pour in the bourbon and ginger ale.

◆ Squeeze the lemon juice into the glass and then toss in the squeezed lemon wedge, stir, and get ready to rumba.

Cocky Cream Soda

Nostalgia gets naughty with this adult version of a childhood classic.

Get It
Ice

2 ounces Stolichnaya Vanil vodka

Coke

Go, Girl

- Fill a rocks glass with ice, add the Stoli Vanil, and pour in some Coke.
- Relive your childhood, only with a warm, fuzzy feeling you never got from your security blanket.

✳ Johnnie Walker Black and Soda

A cute guy I met on Match.com told me this is "a real man's drink." I say it's strong enough for a man, yet made for a woman.

Get It
Crushed ice
2 ounces Johnnie Walker Black Label Scotch whisky
Soda water

Go, Girl
- Fill a rocks glass with crushed ice, add the whisky, and pour in some soda.

✳ Mint Julep

The traditional drink of the annual Kentucky Derby deserves year-round attention. Whether you serve it at brunch, a backyard barbecue, or summer cocktail hour, guests will gallop for refills of this refreshing spring fling, which goes down smooth, yet harnesses the strength and kick of a winning Thoroughbred.

Get It

Fresh mint

1 teaspoon simple syrup* or superfine sugar (available in the baking
section of most upscale grocers)

Crushed ice

2 ounces bourbon (the higher the quality, the better)

To make simple syrup, combine 1 ounce hot water and 2 ounces sugar; chill.

Go, Girl

◆ Crush some of the mint leaves and mix them in a glass with the simple
syrup.

◆ Add the ice and bourbon, and top with a sprig of mint. Giddyup!

Classic Martini

. . . .

Martinis never go out of style. The clincher, especially if you're serving them "up," is the too-cool George Jetson–style glasses. If you don't have martini glasses, this party girl strongly suggests you either opt for another featured libation or serve your martinis on the rocks. But don't furrow your well-tweezed brows if your mind's made up on "up": just serve 'em in small glasses and call them *tackytinis.*

Tips: Make 'em "dirty" with a splash of olive juice to take the hard edge off the straight booze. If you aren't a fan of vermouth, omit it and they're "dry."

Get It
1 splash vermouth
2 ounces gin (or vodka, for a vodka martini)
Ice
1 green olive or lemon twist

Go, Girl
◆ Splash the vermouth into a martini glass and shake the excess out so only what clings to the side of the glass remains.
◆ In a cocktail shaker (or anything makeshift you have around the kitchen), shake the gin with ice like you're Tina Turner.
◆ Strain the gin into the vermouth-blessed glass and top it off with an olive-tipped toothpick or a lemon twist. Cheers!

Manhattan

Like the city it's named after, this classic dark-cherry-colored cocktail seduces with its visuals and flavor and can kick your ass if you're not careful.

Get It
Ice
2 ounces bourbon

1 ounce red vermouth

1 splash angostura bitters

1 maraschino cherry

Go, Girl

◆ Plunk some ice into a mixing glass, pour in the bourbon, vermouth, and bitters, and stir gently until the liquids are chilled.

◆ Drop the cherry into a martini glass, pour the chilled cocktail over it, and play a Frank Sinatra CD.

✳ Lychee Martini

Food & Wine editor in chief Dana Cowin served this rosy and racy elixir at her birthday party. Drop by an Asian market, grab some lychees (small, round fruit popular in Asia), and add an exotic twist to your cocktail party.

Makes 4

Get It

4 teaspoons Chambord (black raspberry liqueur)

4 peeled and pitted fresh lychees or 4 canned lychees

Ice

1 cup vodka, preferably Stolichnaya Oranj

½ cup lychee syrup (from a can of lychees)

Go, Girl

- Add 1 teaspoon of Chambord and 1 lychee to chilled martini glasses.
- Fill a small pitcher with ice. Add the vodka and lychee syrup. Stir well.
- Strain into the martini glasses and serve.

✳ Maui Margarita

When I was a bartender in Hawaii, I lived on this libation. It has all the punch of the traditional tequila concoction plus additional pizzazz in flavor and color. Make it stronger or weaker depending on your intoxication intentions. And hide the blender. This two-toned beauty is served on the rocks. Party tip: Make a potent pitcher and set it out for guests with glasses, ice, a bowl of sliced limes, salt, and cranberry juice.

Get It

3 to 4 ounces limeade (frozen concentrate mixed with water)
2 ounces good to great tequila, more if you're a serious party girl

RAISING THE BAR

Be fashion forward: Serve your own fancy fruit-flavored cocktails by combining vodka, Triple Sec, and any variety of fresh-squeezed juices (your own blend of orange, lemon, pineapple, etc.). Create your own cocktail and start a trend.

½ ounce Triple Sec or Grand Marnier (more if you add extra tequila)
½ lime, cut into wedges
Margarita salt (optional; available at most liquor stores)
Crushed ice
½ ounce cranberry juice

Go, Girl
- Combine the limeade, tequila, and Triple Sec.
- Squeeze the juice from the lime wedges into the mix and throw one squeezed wedge into the batch.
- Moisten the rims of your glasses (pressing them onto a new wet sponge works well) then dip them into a plate of margarita salt. Serve in the salt-rimmed glass over crushed ice, and with a floater of cranberry juice (pour gently so its color doesn't blend with the rest of the margarita).

✳ Bloody Mary

Practically a meal in itself, this rich and red breakfast classic is a health drink playing hooky. It's also well known as a hangover helper, but you don't need to hark the hair of the dog to enjoy this wickedly spicy beverage. However, you may want to clear your schedule if one leads to another. Tip: This recipe serves one, but if you're making more you're best off creating a batch in a pitcher.

Get It
4 ounces tomato juice
1 dash Tabasco

½ teaspoon Worcestershire sauce

½ teaspoon horseradish sauce (or more, if you like it hot)

1 teaspoon lemon or lime juice

1 or 2 shakes of pepper

Salt

Ice

2 ounces vodka

1 celery stick

Go, Girl

◆ Combine the tomato juice, Tabasco, Worcestershire sauce, horseradish sauce, lemon juice, pepper, and salt to taste.

◆ Fill a tall glass with ice. Add the vodka (feel free to pour generously), pour in the tomato juice mix, and garnish with a celery stick.

◆ Serve with a smile.

Mint Condition

Los Angeles caterer Phillip Weingarten didn't serve these when his company, Good Food Catering, presided over Sharon Stone's wedding, but he does serve the perky green drink at Hollywood's hottest summer fetes.

Serves 4

Get It

1 12-ounce can frozen limeade or lemonade

5 ounces vodka

1 handful of fresh mint leaves plus a few sprigs for garnish

Ice

4 lemon wheels

Go, Girl

◆ In a blender combine the frozen limeade, vodka, and mint leaves, and then fill the blender with ice. Blend until smooth or chunky-crunchy, depending on your preference.

◆ Pour the light green libation into glasses and garnish each with a lemon wheel and mint sprigs.

◆ Kermit's wrong. It *is* easy being green.

WHIMSICAL LEMON WHEELS

....

Do this, and your yellow citrus garnishes are gorgeous. First, make your lemon striped lengthwise: With a carefully wielded paring knife, make a flesh-deep cut running lengthwise from the top of the lemon to the bottom. Make another cut, ¼ inch from the first cut. Remember to cut only as deep as the rind. (This is way more difficult to explain than it is to do!) With your fingers or the knife tip, pull away the ¼-inch-wide strip of rind between the two cuts. Repeat to make six equally spaced cuts, all meeting at the top and bottom of the lemon. At this point you should have what looks like a vertically striped lemon. (You can use the discarded strips as twists!) Now slice the lemon widthwise into ½-inch decoratively nobbed wheels. Float the wheels on top of drinks or give 'em a slit and slip 'em onto the rims of the glasses. FYI: This also works with cucumbers and oranges.

✳ Peppermint Stick Martini

Another festive libation from L.A.'s most talented last-minute party boy and caterer, Phillip Weingarten. Try a few of these and you won't even care if you get coal in your stocking this year.

Get It
1 peppermint stick, crushed
1½ ounces vodka
1 ounce peppermint schnapps
1 ounce Triple Sec
Ice
1 small candy cane

Go, Girl
◆ Moisten the rim of a chilled martini glass and dip the wet rim into the pummeled peppermint.
◆ Combine the vodka, schnapps, Triple Sec, and ice in a cocktail shaker.
◆ Shake it like Santa knows you've been bad.
◆ Carefully strain the mix into the martini glass and garnish with the candy cane. Ho ho ho and away we go!

✳ Sour Grape Martini

Pucker up for Phillip Weingarten's sweet-and-sour grape escape.

Get It

1 ounce Grape Pucker (flavored liqueur)

1½ ounces vodka

1 ounce sweet and sour mix

1 ounce Triple Sec

Ice

3 purple seedless grapes

Go, Girl

◆ Combine everything but the grapes in a cocktail shaker.

◆ Then throw your hands in the air and shake your drink like you just don't care.

◆ And if you're not a square from Delaware, serve it up and say "Oh yeah!"

◆ Now would be a good time to bust out your mid-'80s hip-hop albums. Or at least get out a toothpick and garnish your drink with skewered grapes.

Red Hot Martini

Phillip Weingarten turns up the heat with this fiery concoction with a racy red accent.

Get It

1 ounce vodka or, if you like it really hot, Stolichnaya Pepper vodka

1 ounce Goldschläger or De Kuyper cinnamon schnapps

1 ounce simple syrup*

Ice

5 Red Hots or Hot Tamales candies

To make simple syrup, combine 1 ounce hot water and 2 ounces sugar; chill.

Go, Girl
- In a cocktail shaker combine everything but the candy. Shake it like the roof's on fire.
- Pour the mix into a martini glass, toss in the candy pieces, and be cool with your hot stuff.

✳ Bangkoktail

I invented this while whipping up a Thai dinner, and my friends freaked over it. It's decadently dessert-like, dangerously smooth, and has an unexpected hot kick.

Get It
1 ounce vodka
3 ounces canned coconut milk
2 teaspoons sugar
1 kaffir lime leaf, ripped into pieces (optional; available at Thai grocers)
Ice
1 fresh bird's eye chili or other hot chili

Go, Girl
- In a shaker combine the vodka, coconut milk, sugar, kaffir lime leaf, and ice. Shake well and strain into a martini glass.

◆ Slice the hot pepper in half and run the exposed-flesh side around the rim of the martini glass and serve.

✳ Wine Wisdom

No need to get caught up in wine-pairing worries. Even the stuffiest wine aficionados admit that an excellent food-and-wine pairing is food you like with wine you enjoy. Rather than get into nuances that none of your guests are likely to notice as they polish off their second glasses and head for their third, heed a few important rules:

◆ Don't run out. Wine has an astonishing ability to go down smoothly and quickly, so always plan for more than you think you will need. Skimp on provisions and you'll end up rifling through your secret stash and pouring your most prized bottles long after your guests care whether they're drinking the fancy stuff or the corner-store special.

◆ If you want to keep the cost down and your wine supply up, make an event of it. Title your invitation "Show and Tell . . . and Drink" and request that guests bring their favorite wine to share.

◆ Wine rationing is a secret weapon for the pooped party girl. When you're ready for the fete to end, make sure remaining full bottles are out of sight, and let the cups run dry. (Turn off the music, too.) Soon your guests will bid their adieus.

On the occasions that you do want to go the pairing route, don't sweat it. At their core, most pairing philosophies follow one simple guideline:

WINED-UP TOYS

....

"The best $9.95 wine investment you'll ever make is Private Preserve," says master sommelier Evan Goldstein. This nifty tool, which looks like a miniature fire extinguisher, sprays nitrogen into your open wine bottle to preserve the wine months after you've pulled the cork and stuck it back on the shelf. Another favorite: the Rapid Ice Wine Cooler. It's a big, $10 sleeve that you keep in the freezer. It'll chill a bottle of white wine in about 10 minutes, which comes in handy for forgetful party girls who neglected to stick the sauvignon blanc in the fridge. See the Resource Guide on where to find these must-haves for the wine crowd.

Wine characteristics—specifically heaviness and flavor—should be complementary to those in the food. If you're preparing pasta with cream sauce, your wine may be heavier and creamy (think classic California chardonnay). Serving a thick peppery steak? How about a spicy, hearty red. Fish with a squeeze of lemon would marry nicely with a light white that has a lot of citrusy acidity such as sauvignon blanc. The best part? If you don't know or care to know anything about wine, you can go to a wine shop, tell the staff what you're preparing, and ask them to point you toward options in your price range. It's their job to figure this stuff out.

✳

SOMETHING SPECIAL HAPPENS every time I' ve got a feast before me and my friends by my side. Somewhere in between the first cocktail, the toddler taking colored pens to my couch, the impromptu dance party, and sleepy good-byes, I am stopped dead in my twinkle-toed tracks with a private moment of wonder. I look around at the scene I've created, and the magic of entertaining defines itself in one quiet but very powerful instant. Right then I feel full not of the chips, dip, and margaritas, but of the love of friendship. It's this sense of well-being, this celebration of pleasure, people, and good times, that is the party girl's greatest reward. Next time you're mid-fiesta, take a pause and give thanks for your good fortune and friends and your hand in orchestrating one of life's perfect moments. Cheers.

Resource Guide

created this section in case you simply must have something I've mentioned in the book. You can find contact information for products here, as well as go-girl gifts that are sure things in style and taste. Read on for must-haves and shops to which you should turn when it's time to send someone something special.

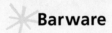

Barware

AMEN WARDY
Caesar's Palace Forum Shops
3500 Las Vegas Boulevard #H03
Las Vegas, NV 89109
877-349-5330 or www.amenwardy.com

This home and gift store with fabulous flair has a presence in Vegas and Aspen, but you can easily shop from home if you've got Internet access. There are plenty of purchase-worthy items for $10 as well as flamboyant furnishings for the more moneyed party girl. Think Diptyque and Votivo candles, X-rated fortune cookies, ultrapampering bath products, all green M&Ms, and colorful cocktail glasses. The Aspen store is at 210 S. Galena Street, Aspen, CO 81611; 970-920-7700.

CRATE & BARREL

800-967-6696 or www.crateandbarrel.com

The national chain hones in on all things for the home, cook, and entertainer with a huge selection of tasteful merchandise and reasonable prices. Shop online, or call or check the Web for a store near you.

POTTERY BARN

888-779-5176 or www.potterybarn.com

With a gazillion stores stocked with affordable classic staples like glasses, dishes, serving utensils and trays, and candles, you can always find something useful to add to your party pantry. Check their site for a store near you, to order a catalog, or to scan their online sales. An added bonus: Last I checked they took phone orders 24-7!

PRIVATE PRESERVE

P.O. Box 2841
Napa Valley, CA 94558
707-252-4258 or www.privatepreserve.com

Private Preserve is a wine-saving wonder that prevents open bottles of wine from going bad for months and even years. Most party girls' fetes end with nothing but empties, but should you want to nurse a bottle or preserve fine cooking oils and vinegars that will otherwise suffer from oxidation, this $9.95 canister of nitrogen is an excellent investment. It should be available at your local fine liquor stores and wineshops, but if not, contact the company's Napa Valley, California, headquarters to find out how to get your hands on it.

URBAN OUTFITTERS

800-282-2200 or www.urbanoutfitters.com

A killer stop for inexpensive and playful decor items. (Think floor pillows, tight tees, dishware, barware, racy rugs, creative lighting, and anything else for the very cool-for-school.) Drop by the website to shop or find the store nearest you.

VACU VIN

415-382-1241 or www.vacuvin.com

The Rapid Ice Wine Cooler by Vacu Vin turns a warm bottle of bubbly or anything else into a cool concoction in about ten minutes. Last checked, the coolers sold for about ten bucks on Amazon.com. You can also ask your local wineshop for one or connect with the manufacturer directly for retailers near you.

WILLIAMS-SONOMA

877-812-6235 or www.williams-sonoma.com

The company has dishware and cooking utensils—much of which you can buy online—but I like to pop in for the $8 peach nectar, which I add to sparkling wine in the summertime.

Candies

RECCHIUTI CONFECTIONS

800-500-3396 or www.recchiuticonfections.com

San Francisco–based chocolatier Michael Recchiuti takes sweets to artistic levels with exotic ingredients in his extremely glamorous gourmet chocolates as well as spectacular candied fruits, s'mores, handmade marshmallows, and brownie packs. They aren't cheap, but in this case money can buy love.

SEE'S

800-347-7337 or www.sees.com

These California-based candy makers have been cranking out classic boxed and individual chocolates since 1921 and still greet visitors with a free piece of something sweet. Whether you buy yourself a treat or send a gift to a friend, don't forget to pocket a posse of lollipops in flavors such as chocolate, butterscotch, and vanilla. Call or go online to order, or check the website for locations in fourteen states.

 # Candles

DIPTYQUE
34, boulevard Saint Germain
75005 Paris
01-43-26-45-27 or www.diptyque.tm.fr

Straight from Paris, perfectly perfumed and decadently refined Diptyque candles and room sprays come in fifty scents sure to burn their way onto your list of must-splurges. The hand-poured seven-ounce glass-encased candles burn for approximately fifty to sixty hours. Rumor has it Sean "P. Diddy" Combs burns fifty of the tuberose scent (one of my personal favorites along with chevrefeuille—a.k.a. honeysuckle—and jasmine) when he's in the recording studio. Room sprays go for about $34. Next time you're in Paris, stock up for half the U.S. price at the Diptyque store. Check the "Address Book" on the website to find the retail outlet nearest you.

VOTIVO, LTD.
206-213-0966

Seattle's finest scented-candle producers design dozens of deliciously scented candles hand-poured into glass jars, distributed nationally, and ranging from the $14, "French jar" version, which burns for about twenty hours, to the larger, $20 size, which burns for fifty hours or more. I'm addicted to Anjou pear and mandarin. Call for local retail outlets or see the Amen Wardy listing under "Barware."

ZINC DETAILS

1905 Fillmore Street

San Francisco, CA 94115

415-776-2100 or www.zincdetails.com

Check out this modern and retro home store for affordable single-flower vases (love the "Flying Saucer" style), incense, distinctive candles, and holders.

Chocolate

RECCHIUTI CONFECTIONS (*See* Candies)

SCHARFFEN BERGER CHOCOLATE

914 Heinz Avenue

Berkeley, CA 94710

800-884-5884 or www.scharffenberger.com

Made in California and boasting a devout national following, this high-quality chocolate should be available in gourmet grocers near you. If not, call the company or visit the website to check the store locator, or have goodies like chocolate baking bars, powder, and cocoa nibs delivered to your door. California-bound chocoholics can tour the factory and buy from the source.

SEE'S (*See* Candies)

SWANSON VINEYARDS
707-967-3500 or www.swansonvineyards.com

Based in California's Napa Valley, Swanson Vineyards is known for its sexy sit-down wine "salon" and tasty wines, but the company also makes a bewitching box of bonbons just right for the go-girl gift. A fabulous hot-pink mini hatbox coddles $35 worth of red-wine-ganache-filled dark chocolate truffles with a sprinkle of curry that sends the gorgeous treat totally over the top. Buy online or call for a box.

Dishware

CRATE & BARREL (*See* Barware)

POTTERY BARN (*See* Barware)

TARGET
800-440-0680 or www.target.com

"Tar-ZHAY" is a go-girl's dream. Stocked with budget-minded must-haves like colorful disposable plates, napkins, and cups and more permanent party fixtures such as chic bathroom accouterments, dishware, chairs, CDs, toys, and everything else you can possibly think of, there's no worries about decorative keepers or trendy impulse buys that are here today, gone-out-of-style tomorrow.

URBAN OUTFITTERS (*See* Barware)

WILLIAMS-SONOMA (*See* Barware)

 Gifts

AMAZON
www.amazon.com

Check out mood music in Chapter 2 and give the gift of grooves.

AMEN WARDY (*See* Barware)

ANTHROPOLOGIE
800-543-1039 or www.anthropologie.com

Appealing to the more feminine gal, this affordable home, clothing, and accessories store offers antiqued furnishings, gorgeously girly tabletop accents, seductive lamps, and all kinds of frilly fun stuff that's great for gifts to yourself or your gal-pals.

CRATE & BARREL (*See* Barware)

DIPTYQUE (*See* Candles)

FRED FLARE
718-599-9221 or www.fredflare.com

For playful and cheap party props (think Superballs, mini accordions, and groovy home decorations) this is a way-cool source.

THE JIMTOWN STORE
6706 State Highway 128
Healdsburg, CA 95448
707-433-1212 or www.jimtownstore.com

Check out the website to send yourself or a pal a tasty gift basket or fantastic fresh spreads. And definitely pop in if you're ever in Sonoma County wine country.

MOMA DESIGN STORE
44 W. Fifty-Third Street
New York, NY 10019
800-447-6662 or www.momastore.org

New York City's Museum of Modern Art brings form and function to gift giving with a delightful selection of toys, home accoutrements, posters, and books starting at around $20. Another New York location is at 81 Spring Street in SoHo (646-613-1367).

P.J. SALVAGE
800-445-6001 or www.pjsalvage.com

This company's gorgeous jammies, camis, Gs, and other intimates are ultimately cute and cozy. A bonus: You can gift one to yourself, and in the event of a surprise slumber party you can seduce someone with your playful bedtime style.

POTTERY BARN (*See* Barware)

RECCHIUTI CONFECTIONS (*See* Candies)

SEE'S (*See* Candies)

SWANSON VINEYARDS (*See* Chocolate)

URBAN OUTFITTERS (*See* Barware)

VOTIVO, LTD. (*See* Candles)

ZINC DETAILS (*See* Candles)

ZIPPER
8316 W. Third Street
Los Angeles, CA 90048
323-951-9190 or www.zippergifts.com

The mod home accoutrements from this fab L.A. store are often featured in *In Style*. Stop here for loads of stylish gifts for a twenty-spot plus shipping.

Home Decor

AMEN WARDY (*See* Barware)

ANTHROPOLOGIE (*See* Gifts)

CRATE & BARREL (*See* Barware)

FRED FLARE (*See* Gifts)

MOMA DESIGN STORE (*See* Gifts)

POTTERY BARN (*See* Barware)

TARGET (*See* Dishware)

URBAN OUTFITTERS (*See* Barware)

ZINC DETAILS (*See* Candles)

ZIPPER (*See* Gifts)

Party Favors

AMEN WARDY (*See* Barware)

FRED FLARE (*See* Gifts)

MOMA DESIGN STORE (*See* Gifts)

Room Spray

DIPTYQUE (*See* Candles)

**Tea**

MIGHTY LEAF TEA
877-698-5323 or www.mightyleaftea.com

The name's goofy, but the teas are anything but. Packed in sexy single-serving mesh pouches pretty enough to put in your underwear drawer, these tasty whole-leaf teas are worlds better than the powdered stuff of yesteryear.

Indexes

* Go-Girl Index

See Recipe Index on page 270

271

272

273

About the Author

ERIKA LENKERT REALIZED the allure of great cooking and entertaining when at eleven years old she could persuade her friends to come over with the promise of homemade garlic bread. By high school she had developed an insatiable desire for eggs Benedict and often found herself whipping up hollandaise sauce in the middle of the night. Through college she accentuated keg parties with homemade sushi or lasagna and worked in restaurants and bars so that she could eat and party her way around the world. Committed to turning her pursuit of pleasure into a career, Erika became a freelance journalist and for a decade has been writing about food, travel, trends, and the good life for everyone from *InStyle*, *Travel & Leisure*, and *Bon Appétit* to *Brides*, *Los Angeles* magazine, and *San Francisco* magazine. She also throws one heck of a party. Today she is probably floating in her pool in Napa Valley, procrastinating on her deadlines, and pulling a roast chicken out of the oven to serve unexpected guests while her two Siamese cats—Caesar and Bailey—kick it in the shade.